CONTENTS

First English edition published by
Kaye & Ward Ltd
194-200 Bishopsgate
London EC2M 4PA
1971

ISBN 0 7182 0812 9

All enquiries and requests relevant to this title should be
sent to the publisher at the above address and not
to the printer.

Printed in Holland by Smeets, Weert.

Gaston Rébuffat

on ice
and snow
and rock

Translated from the French by
Patrick Evans

Kaye & Ward. London

The dream

On the very edge of the world of man, standing upon the summit which had been the magic focus of his dreams, the young mountaineer lifted up his body, his heart, his soul and all his secret longings.

As far as the eye could see a realm of snow and rock lay stretched out before him, wrapped in the silence and mystery of the infinite. It was like being in another world; the mountains seemed less a part of this planet than an entirely independent kingdom, unique and mysterious, where, to venture forth, all that was needed was the will and the love.

Cracks, chimneys, slabs, overhangs . . . The young man had given of his best to climb them. And now he gave himself up to his thoughts, while there mounted within him a happiness such as he had never known before but of which he felt a strange, undefined need. The blood surged through his veins, his heart beat with emotion. The air had a sharp tang, the sun poured out its benediction, and at the end of a rope he had discovered that fine, deep comradeship, the comradeship of climbing companions.

And if mist and cloud obscured the world of other men, then this kingdom was his own for a brief snatch of time, a kingdom to which he was to journey again and again.

He had triumphed over the ground, he had triumphed over himself, and here was heaven's reward for his endeavour.

Youth, to live, must have some great aspiration. When I was fifteen, I was as tall as I am now and thinner; I had little strength in my arms and could pull myself up only with difficulty. Yet I longed so much to become a mountaineer and one day, perhaps, a guide.

Climbing is an instinctive thing. Children clamber spontaneously up window-frames, trees, walls – anything that comes their way. The joy of climbing is the joy of discovery, of being able to see further and from a greater height. Is that not basically what grown-ups call mountaineering? When I was fifteen it was my good fortune that this childhood instinct reawoke in me. Perhaps it was because I grew up in the loveliest playground a child could dream of, a wild desolate place, bounded only by the cliffs and the sea: the Calanques massif, between Marseilles and Cassis.

To become a mountaineer . . .

The 'gendarme' of the Pic de Roc; a very exposed climb. The trickiest part is coming to a standing position at the top: a small ledge hardly wide enough for both feet, and sloping slightly to the right.

I loved the high mountains. Time and time again I had glimpsed them from a valley or a pass or some lowly hilltop, but this satisfied me no longer. I longed to know them, climb them. I had little stamina as yet and realized I must direct my efforts carefully. I lived in Marseilles and periodically felt the need to escape from the city and its din.

In everybody's life there are decisive days, at once happy and lucky. One Sunday in April a friend, my senior by eight years, Henri Moulin, took me climbing in the Calanques, on the Grande Candelle.

I was glad to leave the big city behind me, happy to walk once again along the familiar path. I had come here so often just to look at the Grande Candelle; today I was to climb it. My feelings were a mixture of fear and longing.

We tramped along in silence and deep within me I was aware of a sensation of joy but also of a gripping at my heart. So far I had never been on a rope; I had never done any real climbing; and though this was the moment I had been longing for so much, I was frightened. Moreover, I was overawed by Moulin, despite his kindly manner. He was the expert; he 'knew'. How many successful climbs had he made, how many peaks had he conquered? I had every confidence in him, but it all added up to my being nervous in his company.

At the foot of the face I clumsily uncoiled the rope. At once slightly terrified and slightly excited, I roped up, or rather Moulin roped me up. Then he took the lead. I watched him anxiously as he climbed, until he disappeared round an angle of rock. I realized for the first time what it meant to be on a rope. I tightened my grip on it and when I saw it moving over the surface of the rock wall it took on a great significance. I had understood the beauty of this link.

At last Moulin called me. The rope held. I began climbing, and twice the rope–the friendly extension of Moulin's strong hand–nursed me over a difficult patch.

With some difficulty and with intense joy, I carried on climbing and rejoined him. His confidence had daunted me at first, but now his calm smile reassured me.

With each length of rope this world of rock and silence which I had simultaneously feared and desired became to me a friendly place. I felt that it was moulding me and that for a long time I should belong to it.

Before us lay the sea and the horizon, suggesting the infinity of great spaces; above and below us, the vertical line of great precipices, giving extra depth to the sky. This coming-together of two great realities had an austere simplicity and grandeur; what a starting point for a young man's vocation! An older man was initiating an enthusiastic neophyte and at one stroke throwing open the gateway to my future.

When I got home that night I felt I had found true happiness, happiness of the kind which accorded with my nature. The next day and for some days thereafter I could think of nothing but that first Sunday . . .

Then, gradually, memories of the peaks I had only glimpsed and recollections of this first climb became confusedly intertwined. I began making plans. I thought about acquiring equipment; with my mind's eye I could see it already and I loved it: an ice-axe–my ice-axe –a rope–my rope–my crampons, my rucksack. I looked forward eagerly to setting out for the mountains. I was going to learn the technique not just of climbing, but of mountaineering. Moulin was going to lead me into a world which one can enter only with joy and respect.

Through gates of ice the climber enters the world of the mountains, and the silence and mystery of great heights.

Becoming a mountaineer

To become a mountaineer one must not only learn to climb; one must also learn to understand mountains.

Mountaineering is one of the finest sports imaginable but to practise it without technique is a form of more or less deliberate suicide. Technique promotes caution and, above all, clear thinking; it also obviates fatigue and unnecessary or dangerous halts; and so far from discouraging the contemplative attitude it actually makes it possible. Technique is not an end in itself but the precondition of safety both in the individual climb and on the rope.

The mountains offer us a whole range of pleasures, of which the first is the opening up of a new world of light and silence. The second is perhaps to bring before us a mirror of stone or ice, a mirror which helps us to know ourselves and to become men, as members of the fraternity of the rope. But there are still other pleasures, at once more immediate and more frequent. Doing anything well is always a source of joy.

The joy of climbing well

To climb smoothly, between sky and earth, in a succession of precise, efficient movements, induces an inner peace and even a mood of gaiety; it is like a well-regulated ballet, with every man on the rope in his right place.

A difficulty constitutes a question; the movements which resolve it are the reply. This is the intimate pleasure of communicating with

To study a pitch in advance and foresee the movements dictated by the holds, the climber should incline his body away from the rock face, keeping his hands fairly low.

Artificial aids make it possible to climb a completely smooth wall, provided there is a crack in it. As few pitons as possible should be used, however.

The finest climbing of all will always be free climbing, with just enough holds to render artificial aids unnecessary.
Facing page: The Lépiney crack on the Aiguille du Peigne, a delicate climb, mostly sheer, of great elegance.

the mountain, not with its grandeur and beauty but, more simply, with its material self, its substance, as an artist or craftsman communicates with the wood, stone or iron with which he is working.

Before attacking a crack or chimney the mountaineer looks at it and sums it up squarely, studying its secrets, its good qualities and shortcomings. This is an exciting confrontation; it re-establishes a basic kinship. Then there comes the contact between the rock or ice and the human body. It is pleasant and reassuring to touch a fine piece of granite, or to discover, particularly in limestone, tiny hidden holds which will yield an approach and a way through. How many times have I heard words like these:

'That's an interesting pitch, but is the rock any good?'

'Good solid granite!'

And the climber's face lights up; he sees the lovely colour of the wall, breathes in the smell of the stone, feels the grain of the rock beneath his fingers . . .

Climbs on ice bring other joys; there is an air of unreality as one makes one's way through this land of enchantment, cornices sculpted by the winds, chaotic séracs, finely hemmed arêtes. Getting a good hold with crampons on a steep slope provides a feeling of great serenity; cutting steps neatly and economically brings with it the pleasure of a task well done. To leave a good-looking trail behind one is like leaving one's signature on one's work.

Thus technique resolves problems and brings its own satisfactions.

However, in mountaineering as in other spheres, it remains a poor thing if divorced from the spirit behind it. If the mountaineer climbs only for the sake of climbing he will become deaf to the music he used to hear singing inside him, the music of the mountain's name. But in every man's heart there is always a responsive chord which guides the eager, enthusiastic period of apprenticeship; and after that, the acquired effectiveness itself becomes a thing of beauty. The mountaineer, like practitioners in other fields, has a certain style and though one must not overestimate its importance its presence is a sign of quality; it can be recognized in the distance the climber leaves between himself and the rock face. In climbing, style is intimately bound up with the climber's sense of balance and the sober economy of his performance; then, while his movements follow one another in smooth succession, he is aware of a quiet satisfaction, as if he were receiving a silent approval. Both the climbing and the feeling become like spring-water, which is born of the earth and flows gently, embracing its banks.

Sense of balance

It was in the Dolomites that I first realized the importance of a sense of balance. We were on the north face of the Cima Grande di Lavaredo. Sixteen hundred feet of sheer emptiness! I was happy to be climbing this great wall but glad at the same time to be roped to such a wonderful companion and fine climber, Gino Soldà, a Dolomite guide. I watched him going up ahead of me; what a feast for the eye, and what a lesson! His figure stood out against the sky, a delicate silhouette contrasting with the pure profile of the rock face. Even on the most acrobatic pitches he did not strain; holds seemed to grow beneath his fingers as he made his way up the geometrically vertical precipice with the bearing of a *grand seigneur*.

That day, watching Soldà climb in a style so near to perfection, I came to understand that quite apart from being technically so strong he possessed, completely and in a very precise form, a sense of balance, and that this was the secret of his easy style.

And when we had finished the ascent of the north face and were racing down by the conventional route I continued watching Soldà and confirmed the lesson I had learnt in the morning, and I said to myself over and over again, 'Acquire a sense of balance and you'll climb well. The two things are interdependent.'

To illustrate this point, here are some pieces of advice which I shall develop in the following pages:

On ice, in particular on traverses, repeat without the help of the ice-axe those movements which have been studied with the ice-axe. This is the way to get a good position, with the body held vertically, not leaning against the slope but with the weight directly balanced over the feet.

On rock, the same applies except that the ice-axe is replaced by the handholds. On almost vertical climbs it must be realized that in order to hold oneself to the wall there is no need to hold on tight with the hands, because one's centre of gravity is directly over one's feet and they are enough to carry the whole weight of the body. In other words, the position of a climber on a vertical wall is exactly that of a man standing upright on the floor, except that the climber must brace his feet to take the holds. Thus the novice will become aware that the hands should serve only to maintain the balance of the upper part of the body, both from front to back and from side to side. Contrary to what most people think, the climber does not pull his body up by

1

2

Whenever possible, the climber should raise himself by means of his feet and use his hands only for maintaining balance(1). Sometimes he will have to climb on the layback—a forcible opposition obtained by pulling with the arms and pushing with the feet—while the second climber belays to a rock bollard (2).
Gaston Rébuffat and Maurice Baquet on the south face of the Aiguille du Midi, of which they made the first ascent (3).

the strength of his arms but pushes it up with his legs and feet.

But there is another sort of balance, even more important than physical balance: mental balance.

This is the very keystone of mountaineering, both in the apprenticeship period and in the most advanced climbs. Henri Moulin, Edouard Frendo, André Tournier, Alexis Simond and Marcel Bozon, who initiated me into mountaineering and later into my work as a guide, always taught me this:

'The first thing is always to climb with your head. Know what you want to do and what you're capable of doing. Mountaineering is above all a question of awareness.'

They also told me:

'Take care; too much, even by a fraction, is still too much.'

A climb often has its beginnings in a dream, a moment of exaltation, a spontaneous, sometimes irrational desire; an attractive name, a shape, a story, a memory and there we are, committed to a summit. Then the alluring plan becomes a passionate expectation; preparations begin. But the time comes when it must become a matter of cold calculation; the exact ratio must be found between the *end*— the summit and the route envisaged, conditions of ice and rock according to season, altitude and orientation, and the return route, more or less difficult, on which, in the final analysis, the whole success of the project will depend—and the *means* at the climber's disposal: his capacity for clear thinking, his personal resources (of technique and of mental and physical energy), his knowledge of mountains and weather, his experience and composure.

It is this ratio, *end/means*, which governs decision-making. This formula, unpalatably dry but of fundamental importance, must always be kept in mind by the mountaineer; it determines whether, and when, he sets out. At the moment of decision there is no longer any charm in this world of enchantment, any poetry in this poetic universe; the lives of the mountaineer and his companions may depend on a piece of cold, lucid calculation. And there *is* beauty after all, in this searching dialogue between man and the forces of nature. In the silence of the heights a thoughtful, resolute awareness develops. Fear is just as ugly as rashness is stupid, and can be fatal in its results.

Throughout the ascent the climber is liable to be called upon to revise his judgment in the light of new factors: his degree of tiredness and that of his companions, the time and any delays which may have occurred, snow conditions modified by sun and wind, changes in the weather . . . To give up when close to the top often demands more guts than to go on; conversely, there are times when the only solution is to make a dash for the top to find calmer weather, or an easier way down on the other side.

These compulsory estimates, this clear and definite thinking, so far from impairing enthusiasm, create and support it. A defeat is often more creative than a run of successes. This intimate confrontation between the mountaineer and the world about him, and his resulting involvement, have a quiet grandeur of their own; within the mountaineer, as his self-knowledge and development proceed, is born the man. The mountains are indeed beautiful, but for the time being they become a special setting for an apprenticeship to the craft of living; snow and rock and their partner the sky, together with wind, sun and storm, are moulding two men who have roped up for better or worse, amid snowy solitudes and icy silence.

I think more of a mountaineer for accepting his limitations than for successfully pulling off big exploits. This acceptance is what puts exploits into their true proportions; it means that the climber not

Unlike granite formations, in which fractures in big slabs often show the climber which way to go, other kinds of rock (limestone, gneiss, schists, etc.) give fewer pointers. Sometimes the route appears only after careful search, and a watchful eye is always necessary. These pictures were taken on the Caire de la Cougourde, in the Alpes-Maritimes.

only did something extremely difficult but did it with conscious knowledge. Another thing I appreciate in a climber is his ability to set his passion aside and, in the name of sound judgment, resist his burning ambition to make a fine first ascent. I do not like him to gamble unnecessarily with his life; any fool can do that. In the face of direct danger there is not much to be learned. If a thunderstorm breaks one just takes flight—if one can! It is when considering a difficulty or an obstacle that a man reveals his true stature.

At the bottom of every pitch the mountaineer must study and consider, then climb steadily and calmly, linking his movements smoothly together, reserving his strength and remaining constantly on guard.

Furthermore, an ascent is not only a rock climb or an ice climb but a route to be found, pitches to be linked each to the next, a time-table to adhere to, and the west wind, the storm and darkness to be watched. Thus climbing is only one aspect of mountaineering, just as the climber, properly so called, is only part of the mountaineer. Technique has to be learned, but knowledge of the mountains has to be acquired too. To climb well is fairly easy, finding one's personal equilibrium is harder. The important thing is to get to know oneself; to be invariably capable of summing up the situation without being either nervous or euphoric; to keep one's head well screwed on in any circumstances; and never to confuse those two very different notions, danger and difficulty. The first is morbid, the second healthy and virile. Mountaineers love beauty, comradeship and life; these are what they respect, not a taste for taking silly risks.

The reward waiting for the mountaineer at the summit is a quiet serenity and the opportunity to contemplate an almost endless horizon. If he had been dropped there from an aircraft the view would be the same but would seem less lovely to him; the pillars of our sport are exertion and comradeship. 'In order to see—really see—it is not enough to open your eyes, you must begin by opening your heart.'

The Grande Gendarme, on the Grépon (above), provides a difficult, dizzying climb, with few holds but very sound rock. The hands should be kept low, even if the climber is tall.

The rules of the game

In mountaineering, the storm that blows up unexpectedly, the cold that freezes you and the wind that doubles you up, the slope that threatens to avalanche, the *verglas*, the mist or even just the fall of darkness, all form part of the rules of the game just as much as dry, warm rock or firm ice in which the crampons bite securely. Hence the mountaineer's technique must be adequate to diminish the effect of any unfavourable conditions, and his clothing and equipment must be first-class.

One might almost say the mountaineer should choose a freezing cold day, with the rain coming down in buckets, on which to go shopping for his outfit. Perhaps this would make him more certain to choose sound warm clothes and enable him to imagine the qualities his equipment simply must possess, though of course bad weather in a town is nothing compared with a storm at 14,000 feet!

In the mountains you can set out in sunlight, only to find the weather deteriorating at some point in the climb. It may start snowing, visibility may decrease and the cold become paralysing. More than once I have known the temperature at 14,000 feet drop from 85°F (30°C) to −5°F (−20°C) in a couple of hours.

If a crampon strap breaks, or merely comes undone, the climber has to stop. He tries to fasten it but cannot; his mitts make his hands clumsy so he has to remove the mitts, taking great care not to lose them; if he simply puts them down they will slip away into the void; if he sticks them in the ground they will fill with snow. The slope is steep, the snow eddies around, the wind is violent and icy-cold. On touching the snow his bare fingers go numb, and the intense cold makes them stick to the metal clasps. The frozen strap has stiffened and refuses to slip through the metal ring, and the buckle is coated with ice.

Even if the climber succeeds in keeping perfectly calm his movements become awkward and fumbling, his fingers disobey him; he has to clap them into life again and then warm them against his body.

Ascent of the Aiguille du Midi via the Arête des Cosmiques, ending in a very short climb presenting no great difficulties. In the background, Mont Blanc (1).

Bivouac at 13,000 feet on the Walker Spur, on the north face of the Grandes Jorasses (2).

Bad weather over the Aiguilles de Chamonix (3).

Bivouacking in hammocks—on the Capitan, a lofty granite wall in the Yosemite National Park, USA. Slung from pitons the nylon hammock makes it possible to bivouac fairly comfortably on sheer faces without a ledge anywhere.

Time is passing and the storm becoming fiercer, eddies of snow lash his face and pierce him through and through; every gust peels another layer of warmth from him. It is in such circumstances that a tiny incident can become an accident, and, if it is late in the day, necessitate a dangerous bivouac.

Bivouacking

Bivouacking is a good thing to learn, primarily as a matter of technique and safety. If you know what bivouacking is like, what it means to spend a night at a high altitude, which is the coldest part of the night and which hour passes slowest, you will not feel helpless if, through chance or circumstance, you find yourself forced to bivouac. An ordeal you have previously undergone is by so much the less to be feared.

The pleasure of bivouacking is another reason for learning; a virile pleasure because of the cold and lack of comfort, and also a means of getting to know the mountains better and acquiring a deeper experience of altitude, a sense of its meaning. The mountaineer who restricts himself to fine weather or climbs only from a hut experiences the splendour of the mountains but not their mystery, the approach of which coincides with that of darkness. There are some aspects of our sport that reveal themselves only to the man who bivouacs, with his back against the rock-face and his mind open to a kind of meditation which is the prolongation of the climb itself.

Certainly the climber is surrounded by the silence of the heights by day, but at that time he has other things to do besides listen to it; he is immersed in activity. At night he stops perforce and is free to put himself into harmony with the rock, and with the snow which moves not at all or, at most, shifts imperceptibly. There may indeed, when the temperature drops after a thaw, be a sudden loud noise, an avalanche, say, or a sérac toppling over, but this is only a momentary disturbance; night in the mountains is a time of peace; the sun fading; the stars blossoming briefly only to die when the light returns in the opposite quarter of the sky and, with the light, the warmth to which your flesh responds.

Some of my friends are proud of having made all their ascents without a single bivouac. But while their technique is beyond criticism and their speed has often provided a potent safety-factor, I think they have deprived themselves of something essential. We are deprived of so many things in life by the way we have to live it; why add to their number?

I have often bivouacked, and there are plenty of different ways of doing it: lying, sitting or standing, asleep or awake, happy or anxious, in calm or stormy weather, for pleasure or of necessity. In fact, bivouacking is like so much else in life!

On the Grand Capucin, during one of the early rehearsals (the fourth, if I remember rightly) for Bonatti's ascent, I spent the night, in rough cold weather, standing in the stirrups—sometimes more or less sitting in them, but they were too narrow and cut off the circulation in my legs, which went heavy and as if dead. I shall always remember that night. But I also remember bivouacking on purpose, one calm evening, at the top of the Matterhorn. The endless strings of noisy climbers on the Swiss and Italian arêtes had departed. My

The sun is about to set behind the Matterhorn. On the right: the Hornli arête (the Swiss arête); upper left: the Furggen arête, with the shoulder of the arête du Lion (the Italian arête) below it; the shoulder is also known as Tyndall's peak. Extreme left: the Dent d'Hérens.

two companions and I were alone on the summit; silence had returned in twofold measure—because we were alone and because we had stopped climbing—so that it acquired a new density and the Matterhorn itself an added dimension; the mountain seemed even bigger than it had been five years earlier, when we had bivouacked not under a clear sky but in a fearful storm of thunder and lightning. On that occasion, despite having stopped climbing, we were still, in effect, active and under tension, as if scaling a difficult face; 500,000 volts were playing all around us. But on the night when we bivouacked from choice we felt receptive not to some communication from the beyond but, more directly, to the very nature of the Matterhorn; we were part and parcel of its rock and snow as one is of one's own home country. Say, if you like, that this was all in the mind (certainly the mountain itself was not changed in any way by our spending the night on its summit), and that the bivouac was merely an amusement; nevertheless the fact remains that we were glad to be there or, more precisely, to be there not by mistake but on purpose, so that we were not an alien element in the scene nor mere spectators of it. And we experienced a happiness which we could not have felt by day.

There are climbers who will not even hear of making a bivouac. But those who have tried it once find that the experience has an unforgettable flavour. I am far from being alone in my attitude; here is just one example. A few years ago, when I was on a lecture tour in the United States, a small party was arranged for some climbers. One of them made straight for me and said, 'I know you like bivouacs. So do I.' He was Yvon Chouinard, who had made a number of notable first ascents and is now a well-known manufacturer of excellent pitons. We spent some time discussing technique and climbers' hardware, naturally, and we also talked about bivouacking; but then the talk slowed down and we became meditative, partly because language is a slippery medium and the exact words for pinning something down are hard to find, but also because happiness eludes expression anyway; and, again, because men are reticent about expressing their emotions and their feelings for beauty, so that one naturally falls back on discussing pitons. Roughly, our conversation was an epitome of the contents of this book.

On Ice and Snow and Rock is not for the top-flight performer but the beginner. It will give him pointers on technique—the technique I apply in my own climbs. Still more, it will attempt to convey an attitude, an approach to mountaineering, an initiation into the spirit of the heights.

Clothing and equipment

When acquiring clothes and equipment it is essential to think of their likely performance in storm conditions, and always to choose the best.

In practice, moreover, clothes and equipment must always be those best suited to whatever expedition has been planned. Obviously they will not be the same for climbing Mont Blanc by the normal route as by the difficult Peuterey arête, which may necessitate a bivouac; or for the easy, sunlit south face of the Cima Grande di Lavaredo as by the severe, overhanging north face. On the other hand, it should always be borne in mind that changes in weather and temperature can take place very suddenly in the mountains. The mountaineer, while avoiding unnecessary weight, must provide adequately for all eventualities. His clothing should be such that he can always quickly take some off or put more on.

When packing your rucksack, take as little as possible: weight is the enemy. On the other hand, don't forget anything. Every item of clothing and equipment must be chosen carefully for the particular climb you are undertaking; approximations won't do, whether on ice, snow or rock, using natural means or artificial aids; (left-hand page) include a double rope, pitons, snap-links and stirrups.

Formerly, soft, supple boots, or even espadrilles, were worn, and the technique used was resistance, i.e. pushing with the feet and pulling with the hands. But now, thanks to rigid boots with 'armed' soles, even the smallest holds can be utilized; the weight of the body is supported by the feet, the chief function of the arms being to maintain the balance of the upper part of the body.

Equipment may come under severe strain at any time and should be in perfect condition at the start of every trip. The smallest details are important. There should be no boots, breeches or windjackets with stitching coming apart, no Vibram soles coming unstuck, no pullovers, jackets or socks too short. The slightest oversight, such as a glove with a hole in one fingertip, or a broken bootlace, could lead to serious trouble.

To be sure of one's equipment is a safety measure, and to feel comfortable in one's clothes an added source of pleasure.

CLOTHES

These must be very warm and strong, but light in weight. Clothes should not hamper movement or restrict circulation.

Clothes, etc., for walking and climbing

Stockings should be of wool and come up to the knees so that there is no gap between breeches and stocking when the leg is raised. For some snow expeditions two pairs of stockings are worn, one pair of which should be of fine wool.

Boots. These should have the minimum number of seams, and the inner surface of the sole should fit the arch of the instep to minimize fatigue. There should be a decided hollow for the climber's heel to fit into, so that it does not rub up and down inside the heel of the boot. If the boots are too roomy and the feet 'float' in them there will be friction and overheating and blisters will result. For the same reason, the boots should not be done up too loosely, even on the approach march. The opening and lacing of the boot should extend almost to the toe, so that the feet can be inserted easily even when the boots are hard or, as is the case sometimes when preparing to start in the morning, frozen; another advantage is that the front part of the foot can be held as closely as one likes by the boot, giving a better purchase on small holds. The boots should also be 'armed'; the sole, that is, should be laminated internally with a strip of steel to make it rigid, so that, without much muscular contraction and fatigue on the part of the toes, foot and leg, the tip of the boot provides a secure purchase on even the smallest holds. For the same reason the sole should not project too far; the narrower the welt, the less the leverage, hence less fatigue and greater security on small holds.

Boots always used to be nailed, with clinkers or Tricounis. But for the last thirty years nailing has been rightly abandoned in favour of Vibram soles, invented by a Milanese mountaineer, Vitale Bramani. This invention has considerably increased both the pleasure and the safety of climbing; it has also brought an improvement in technique, since whereas clinkers or Tricounis could be fixed only on a projecting sole, Vibram soles require no such change of outline, thus fulfilling the essential need that the climber's toes should be as close to the rock as possible.

When the first Vibram soles appeared everyone thought they would be a great improvement for rock climbing, but many mountaineers were afraid there would be a corresponding disadvantage on snow, where rubber soles might slip. But this is not the case: Vibrams are 'treaded' in such a way that they hold well on snow. On

ice, it is another matter; clinkers and even Tricounis are inadequate, and the only solution is to put on crampons.

Finally, Vibrams are lighter than nailed soles, less tiring, especially during the descent, and silent.

It is a good thing to have different boots for different types of climb: a light pair for climbing on limestone, a medium pair for rock climbing at high altitudes, and warmer, thicker ones for winter climbing or any long ascent on snow.

Gaiters. In the last few years gaiters have come back into fashion in mountaineering and elsewhere. They are useful in really deep snow and keep the legs pleasantly warm, but sometimes make the feet cold: a little snow tends to make its way up between the top of the boot and the edge of the gaiter, and stay there. In all other conditions, it seems to me that 'stop-touts', which are lighter into the bargain, are enough.

Stop-touts. These are much to be preferred to the gaiters or puttees which were used at one time. A stop-tout is a muff of proofed material, elasticated at both ends and giving perfect waterproof protection. Stop-touts are effective against snow and even keep out bits of grit on the approach march or on descents over screes or in stone gullies.

Over-boots are waterproof bags, of approximately the same shape as boots, worn over the boots proper and giving excellent protection.

Breeches. These should be of the knickerbocker or short plus-four type, that is to say extending only about 4 inches below the knee. Avoid plus-fours which are too long or too full, as they get wet in the snow and the crampons get caught up in them. The breeches may be of corduroy or light-weight gaberdine for rock climbing, especially in the Dolomites, and absolutely must be of strong warm cloth (Grenfell Bonneval or Bagnes) for high-altitude climbs and particularly for ice work.

Trousers of stretch material are pleasant to wear, since despite their shortness they do not hinder the bending of the knee (mountaineers who are also skiers often use an old pair of 'drainpipes').

There are also special kinds of trouser: quilted trousers for expedition work or winter climbing, nylon mesh over-trousers to go with quilted trousers or worn outside breeches for climbing on snow at high altitudes or in intense cold.

Long underpants. Made of wool, silk or rhovylon; used on north faces or in long climbs over snow.

Shirt. This should be very warm, therefore of wool, especially for long climbs. It should be long enough not to come out of the breeches when the climber raises his arms.

Sweater. This should be long enough to cover the stomach and loins.

Duvet (quilted jacket). This is not always necessary but, considering its negligible weight (700 or 800 grammes; well under 2 lb) and small size when neatly folded, it is always a pleasant thing to have, ensuring a comforting warmth. But it must be of high quality; which means:

The nylon cloth must be of a close weave, especially made for the purpose; and while it must have been given an 'anti-down' treatment (to stop the stuffing percolating through the material) this must not prevent the down from 'breathing'.

The stuffing must be genuine white or silver-grey goose down, which is not easy to come by, and during manufacture the weight of

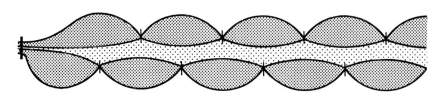

Cross-section of part of a double-walled quilted jacket.

Gloves and mitts are used when climbing on snow or ice—they are seen here in conjunction with a hold cut on a very steep slope; also for running belays; and sometimes on rock, if the temperature is very low (1).

In the short passages of rock climbing that sometimes punctuate a climb on snow, the best way to carry the ice-axe is to slip it between the back and the rucksack. This is a time-saver; the ice-axe can be slipped in or out in a moment. If delays are avoided in managing the rope and other equipment, more time will be left for making a leisurely halt at the summit and getting the most out of the climb (2).

The rucksack, whether small or large, should be on the lines of the peasant basket (3).

the stuffing must be controlled by photo-electric cell to ensure that the amount is correct and the distribution regular.

Two-skin construction is the only way of avoiding loopholes for the cold to get in by, and has the further advantage of providing an extra layer of air for insulation. A sectional view of this construction makes its advantages clear.

Finally, as the above drawing also shows, a quilted jacket of this type is, putting it simply, two such jackets sewn together, one inside the other, with the seams staggered.

Anorak. This should be of strong, tightly woven, waterproofed poplin or Grenfell cloth, with hood and pockets. Every mountaineer develops his own habits. Some prefer climbing in a comparatively light sweater and a heavy anorak, others in a thick pullover and, if conditions are cold or windy, an anorak of lightweight nylon, taking care however always to have, in the bottom of the rucksack, a 'bivouac cagoule' in case the weather turns nasty. The most important thing is that all these clothes—shirt, sweater, anorak and quilted jacket—should come down well below the waist, so that whenever the climber has to raise his arms, inevitably pulling up the clothes in question, his abdomen and the small of his back are still protected. For the same reason, it is advisable that trousers be kept up with braces.

Cagoule. Pierre Allain has evolved a long cagoule in waterproofed fabric, known as the 'bivouac cagoule'; he used it successfully as early as 1935, on the north face of the Drus, and on all his major climbs. Like Vibram soles, the bivouac cagoule is an invention which has given markedly increased protection against bad weather and accidents and has undoubtedly saved the lives of mountaineers caught in storms. Originally made of rubberized fabric but latterly of waterproofed nylon, the bivouac cagoule weighs little and folds small; every mountaineer should have one in his rucksack, for quite apart from bivouacs he will find it very helpful whenever the weather breaks and the thermometer goes down: in rain, snow, cold or wind. Another arrangement, equally good, is to have a normal-length cagoule of waterproofed nylon and trousers of the same material, so that the lower legs are protected too. The trousers can also be used as overtrousers in long climbs on snow. This is a practical, lightweight outfit.

Gloves and mitts. Mitts keep the hands very warm as the fingers remain in contact, but gloves allow greater precision. Gloves should be oiled wool or waterproofed leather. Mitts can be of either of these materials, or of cloth or even duvet.

For high-altitude snow work it is a good idea to wear gloves of fine wool, or silk if you prefer it, with mitts outside them; or else cloth or nylon mitts with a nylon fur lining, of 'Makalu' type, which give excellent protection against very cold powder snow.

1

Headgear. Every man to his taste. The important thing is to keep the ears and sinuses well protected. A peak is useful in bright sunlight or in snow or rain. At high altitudes a Balaclava helmet is essential.

Crash helmet. A crash helmet is in every way an unpleasant thing to wear, primarily because it hints at the possibility of an accident: a fall or glissade in which the climber lands on his head; falling stones or icicles, which can be lethal; or an avalanche. These things can and do happen. The use of crash helmets ought to become universal.

A helmet should (a) resist impact and crushing–the shell must be strong, yet neither too rigid in itself nor too rigidly attached to the head; (b) act as a shock-absorber, so that the force of an impact is not transferred to the skull and cervical vertebrae–this is a matter of the lining and its support and shows that the inside of the helmet is as important as the outside. The lining and its support must rest evenly on the climber's head and leave a space of at least 3 cm (1·2 ins) between the scalp and the inner surface of the shell.

Goggles. These should protect the eyes completely, even at the sides. Mica is not enough; filter lenses are essential. When not in use goggles should be kept in a metal case, otherwise you may find them broken just when you need them. A case of opthalmia is a serious accident.

Rucksack. This used to be in the shape of a pear hanging down the climber's back, forcing him to lean forwards to compensate for the weight hanging low behind. Some twenty years ago a new type was evolved, of the opposite shape, wider at the top (both from front to back and from side to side) than at the bottom; this was based on the basket used by the peasants in Savoy and elsewhere (which enables a man to carry 160 lb of potatoes without being thrown off balance) and on the 'hooks' used by the men who provision the mountain huts. The 'hook' is a tall frame on which the load rests; it causes the weight to be taken not low down but above the waist. The same principle is found in the carrying-frame used for portage in the American wilds.

At the present time there are various kinds of rucksack, all based on the same design. Unfortunately, however, there is frequently a tendency to seek greater effectiveness by cluttering the ideal shape with redundant features; it is too seldom remembered that perfection occurs not when there is nothing to add, but nothing to take away. One useful feature is a pocket on the back flap.

For mountain skiing, pockets at the sides are a necessity, especially as they constitute guides through which the skis can be slipped for carrying when not in use.

One always tends to take too large a rucksack. What matters is to pack it carefully; it is surprising how much can be got in. It is simply a question of being methodical and acquiring the habit. The smaller the rucksack and the less it juts out beyond the outline of the mountaineer's back, the lighter it will seem, even though heavily loaded, because the weight will be close to the back and shoulders.

Bivouac rucksack. This is the same shape as an ordinary rucksack but has an extension as tall as the sack itself. During the climb the extension remains inside; when you want to bivouac you pull it out, and the two parts together protect the lower part of your body almost up to the waist.

Things which should always be in a mountaineer's rucksack: A spare pair of mitts, stockings, goggles and bootlaces; a first-aid

2

3

outfit, two or three pitons, 5 yards of line, an altimeter and, for certain climbs, a compass, map and guidebook.

Altimeter. A very useful accessory on big climbs. For the past three years the Société Favre-Leuba, Geneva, has been manufacturing a watch embodying a high-precision barometer and altimeter.

Headlamp. The old-fashioned candle lantern, attractive but inconvenient, has been replaced by the electric torch, and particularly by a torch strapped to the forehead, which has the double advantage of throwing a more effective beam and of leaving the hands free. It is better to fix the battery-case to the elastic band round the head than to have it in a pocket, with a lead to the torch; the flex might get in the way or catch on something.

Bivouac equipment

This must be at once efficient and very light.

Cagoule. The one already recommended for ordinary work. Make sure it is long enough; it must come down well below the knees.

'Elephant's foot'. This is an extension of the cagoule and is made of the same waterproofed material. Its purpose is to protect the thighs, calves and feet.

Quilted jacket. I must stress once again that it must be a good long jacket, not a shirt stopping short at the waist.

Short, down-filled sleeping-bag. For some climbs and bivouacs it is useful to have a down sleeping-bag of less than the normal length. It should come up only to the chest, particularly as some of the models now available are extremely light and pack very small. The quilted jacket and sleeping-bag, plus the cagoule and elephant's foot, make excellent bivouac gear; possessing, however, the combined advantage and disadvantage of being an individual outfit, and therefore suitable for bivouacs in which the individuals' positions are small and separate.

The Zdarsky bivouac bag. This is a sort of folding sack-tent made of waterproofed nylon. It has the advantage of sheltering two mountaineers at once, so that they share each other's warmth. Its

Gaston Rébuffat and Haroun Tazieff have just passed the rocky hummock on which the Vallot hut stands (right-hand page). The Chamonix valley can be seen far below, the Les Fiz range in the background, and the Dôme du Goûter to the left. The handle of a shovel protrudes from Tazieff's rucksack; the two climbers are going to spend the night in an igloo on the top of Mont Blanc.

Here, Tazieff is looking out from the mouth of the igloo they have built.

32

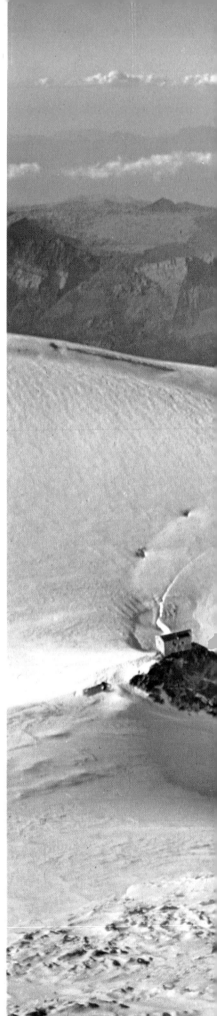

drawback is that they have to have enough room to be side by side. If they bivouac in the sitting position their heads, facing each other, act as tent poles, unless the Zdarsky is hitched by the two loops at the top corners to pitons fixed in the rock-face just above the ledge where the bivouac is made. The Zdarsky give good protection against snow, wind and loss of warmth. There are several variations of the Zdarsky but they all work on the same principle.

Hammock. This is made of nylon netting and is slung from pitons, enabling one to bivouac fairly comfortably, even on the steepest rock-faces.

Alpine tents. These give a certain amount of comfort and, what matters more, good protection against cold and storms. They have saved the lives of a number of mountaineers in the summer and even more in winter, especially on long winter climbs requiring at least two days and sometimes more, because of bad weather.

CLIMBING EQUIPMENT

The rope

Hemp and manilla have been eclipsed by nylon (or perlon), the advantages of which are beyond argument.

Nylon is waterproof and does not rot. Nylon ropes are as supple when wet as when dry, unlike hemp and manilla which, when wet, become stiff, difficult to handle and run very badly in the snap-links in belaying or abseiling. Nylon fibre absorbs neither water nor water-vapour, and when a nylon rope is wetted the water runs off it easily.

Nylon is light. For a given diameter, nylon weighs only from 10 to 20 per cent less than hemp, but for a given breaking strain the weight of nylon is only 50 per cent of that of hemp.

Nylon is much better at absorbing a sudden strain. When you think of it, a fall when climbing, especially on the part of the leader, is a source of energy, and arresting the fall involves the problem of absorbing this energy. The introduction of nylon–a fairly elastic synthetic fibre, certainly much more elastic than hemp–has focused attention on a factor which, though already known, had never been exploited in the interest of safety, namely that the considerable lengthening undergone by the rope when subjected to a sudden pull absorbs energy; so much so that our ideas on protection against falls have been transformed, permitting considerable advances not only in material and equipment but in technique and safety.

In 1958 the journal of the Club Alpin Français, *La Montagne,* published an extremely important article by Professor Dodéro on 'The Unknown Factor: The Rope' ('Les cordes, ces inconnues'). Coming after more than a century of mountaineering, this penetrating article was enough to give one cold shivers down the back. Ropes had always previously been classified according to their breaking strains, a static measure determined by the amount of weight at rest required to break a given rope; but since a fall is, by definition, dynamic, this was obviously fairly meaningless. Dodéro devised an apparatus for testing dynamic resistance, reproducing in the laboratory the nature of an actual fall in climbing. The rope was always subjected to two shocks, not one, so as to make sure that it was not seriously weakened by a single fall. Each shock simulated the fall of a climber weighing 80 kilos (about 190 lb), represented by

2

a weighted motor-tyre, from a point some 30 feet above his companion and 8 feet above a snap-link. The most unexpected of the results, the spine-chilling part, was the revelation that a rope of natural fibre, even with a high breaking strain, was weak, vulnerable, virtually ineffective: 'The shock causes a miniature explosion in the form of a little cloud of hemp.' A few synthetic fibre ropes were the only ones to stand up to the tests and to be awarded the quality label of the F.F.M. (Fédération Française de la Montagne). Dodéro's apparatus has since been modified and improved so as to measure the maximum tolerable remainder, the residual amount of impact which the climber could stand after the main part of the force had been absorbed by the stretching of the rope. The point being that not only must the rope arrest the fall, but also that the climber must not be injured or killed by too violent a check. As the opposite extreme to hemp ropes, which snapped almost like glass, we may postulate an unbreakable steel cable; but obviously the climber's body would then be more or less cut in half by the sudden pressure of the cable.

In climbing, every movement must be exact; this is true not only of the hands but at least equally so of the feet, which then, even on the tiniest holds, become capable of bearing the climber's whole weight (1).

The technique for descending a vertical or overhanging rock-face is roping down (abseiling); if properly carried out this is a perfectly safe method, but the slightest negligence can make it highly dangerous (2).

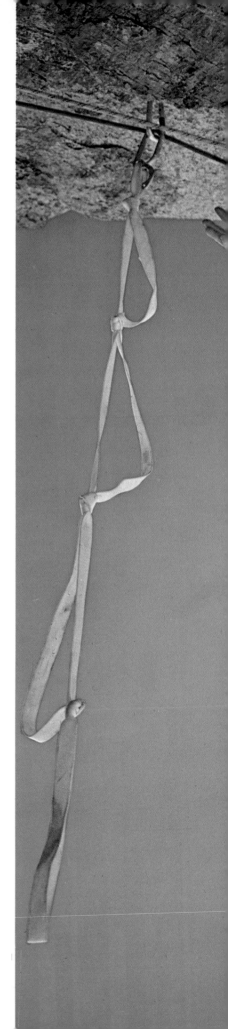

Both the F.F.M.'s label and that of the Union Internationale des Associations Alpines (which has of course concerned itself with this fundamental question) cover a number of requirements (flexibility of the rope, degree of stretching allowed, good handling qualities, freedom from kinking, resistance to wear, ability to shed water and humidity, behaviour at low temperatures, resistance to atmospheric conditions). Both labels constitute an assurance of high quality, though not an absolute guarantee against breakage.

Today's mountaineers, whether they know it or not, go climbing with incomparably better ropes than their predecessors, an advantage won for them by Professor Dodéro's investigations and the continual, patient, persevering work of the F.F.M. and latterly of the U.I.A.A.: both these organizations are still studying this question, the importance of which is of the first order.

Hemp ropes, being subject to rotting, should be of twisted, not plaited, construction, so that their condition can always be checked. In plaited ropes the core is protected by the sheath from friction against the rock and can fray unseen; meanwhile the sheath may also fray fairly quickly.

In twisted ropes, direct wear occurs on all three strands; but despite being worn on the surface they may retain a good deal of strength internally.

When belaying, and in particular when holding a fall, one can get more purchase on a twisted rope, whose surface is in relief, than a plaited one, which is smooth. But against this, a plaited rope is suppler and easier to handle than a twisted one. At the present time the great majority of ropes are plaited.

The main types of rope and their uses are as follows:

The single rope (11 mm diameter); this is for the team rope or connecting rope and is used only for this purpose.

The double rope (9 mm diameter); this is for roping down and can also be used double as the team rope. Ropes of this diameter are two-coloured (one colour at one end, the other at the other) so that the middle is always easy to find; this is convenient both for abseiling and when roping up.

The length of the rope depends on the climb: 60 to 65 feet between each climber for normal climbs, about 100 feet for very ambitious projects and about 130 feet for very long pitches. For double ropes these lengths must of course be multiplied by two.

Thinner ropes are also used, of 7 mm diameter, for roping down (occasionally, not as the regular thing) and for hauling up the rucksacks when necessary.

Line and webbing. Finally, there is 5 mm line for making étriers and abseil slings, and the nylon webbing which was introduced by the Americans about 1960 and which is a great help at times, provided you know how to use it: being very thin, it will slip through places where line will not; and being flat and broad, it will hold on an almost imperceptible rock bollard where line, being round and able to roll about its longitudinal axis, would slip off. Webbing can of course also be used for making abseil slings and étriers without platforms. It is made in two widths, approximately 13 and 26 mm, capable of supporting 700 kilos (1,540 lb) and 1,900 kilos (4,180 lb) respectively. It is always useful to carry half a dozen webbing slings of different lengths.

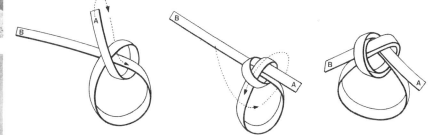

Knot for making abseil sling from a length of nylon webbing.

Care of ropes. Unlike ropes made from natural fibre, synthetic fibre ropes need no maintenance. They dry quickly; the only precautions necessary are to avoid exposing them to heat or bright light,

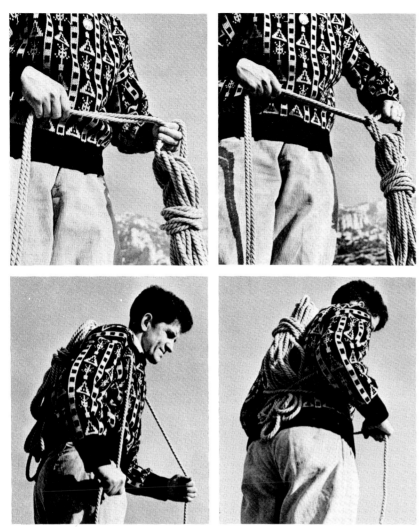

The advantage of skein coiling is that it makes the ropes easy to carry, both when climbing and when roping-down.

and coiling them on too tight a radius; and no rope should ever be trodden on, even with Vibram soles. To 'stop' the ends of a nylon rope (i.e. to prevent fraying) simply heat them until the fibres melt sufficiently to weld together. Finally, it is obvious that the rope of which one no longer feels sure should be discarded without hesitation.

Coiling the rope. This must be essentially practical. The climber should be able to coil or uncoil his rope quickly even in a very confined space; on a narrow ledge, for instance.

Skein coiling. This is the most practical method. There is no need whatsoever to find the middle to start coiling; it is just as easy to begin at the ends. Make neat, equal loops; not too long, however, or the rope will tend to catch on the rock when it is being carried slung over the shoulders and the climber is making his descent facing outwards.

Having made all the loops, wind the free ends (both together) round them as high up and as tightly as possible; after which there are two alternatives, according to taste: either pass both free ends through the upper bend of the loops; or make a loop of the free ends together, pass it through the upper bend of the main loops, bring it back over the top of the bend and pass the free ends through it.

In either case there are 10–12 feet of rope left over which can be turned into braces, so that the rope can be carried slung over the shoulders.

If one knows in advance that more than one abseil will be required it is better to make two skeins, each of single rope and consisting of half of the whole rope; an easy matter, the rope being two-coloured. On reaching the place where the abseil is to begin, the whole of one skein is passed through the sling; this saves time in a manoeuvre which is always tedious.

Other methods of coiling are now mainly of antiquarian interest; this even applies to crown coiling, which is rather slow and decidedly less convenient than skein coiling.

The baudrier or shoulder-harness. Increasingly, climbers are using a baudrier or shoulder-harness instead of roping-up directly on to the rope. This is all to the good, but it should be noted that a baudrier *must* be complete: it must consist not only of the belt and the upper braces passing over the shoulders, but also of the lower braces passing under the thighs. This one-piece device, in which all the straps are fastened together, does not merely hold the mountaineer but carries him, in much the same way as a parachutist is carried by his harness. This is important: it greatly reduces fatigue in artificial climbing and on acrobatic pitches with scanty holds; and it is doubly important in the case of a fall, when the climber concerned is dangling over empty space.

The chief requirement in a baudrier is that the stitching must be at least as strong as the straps themselves.

The ice-axe

This is at once the mountaineer's tool and his closest companion. It is used: (a) as a stick or prop on snow slopes, ice slopes and arêtes, and for sounding snow bridges to test their strength; (b) in negotiating bergschrunds, when it can be driven in to provide a hold. Some guides even used to use it successfully on rock, to provide a jammed hold; (c) for cutting steps.

An ice-axe consists of a *handle,* one end of which is enclosed in a steel ferrule terminating in a *spike;* the other end is held between two *tongues* which carry the *head;* one end of the latter is shaped like a *pick* and the other like an *adze.* The pick is provided with notches to make it hold better when driven into ice. These well-defined notches serve their purpose excellently, especially when the ice-axe is being used in the 'anchor' position, but this advantage becomes a handicap when cutting is necessary; they do not hinder the cutting effect itself but they do impede withdrawal – the point tends to stick in the ice just when you want to free it and carry on cutting.

The head of the ice-axe may be pierced with holes: one parallel to the axis of the handle, to take a snap-link so that the ice-axe can be hooked on to an ice-screw, or hung at one's waist; two in the blade, through which the adze or pick of another ice-axe can be inserted to support a climber in negotiating a difficult place, for example on a bergschrund.

The handle is oval in section and is made of straight-grained ash,

Technique, material and equipment enable puny human beings to advance safely and enjoyably along arêtes which have been delicately hemmed by the winds.
Below, the Glacier du Géant; background, the Col du Géant, the Dent du Géant, the Arêtes de Rochefort and Mont Mallet.

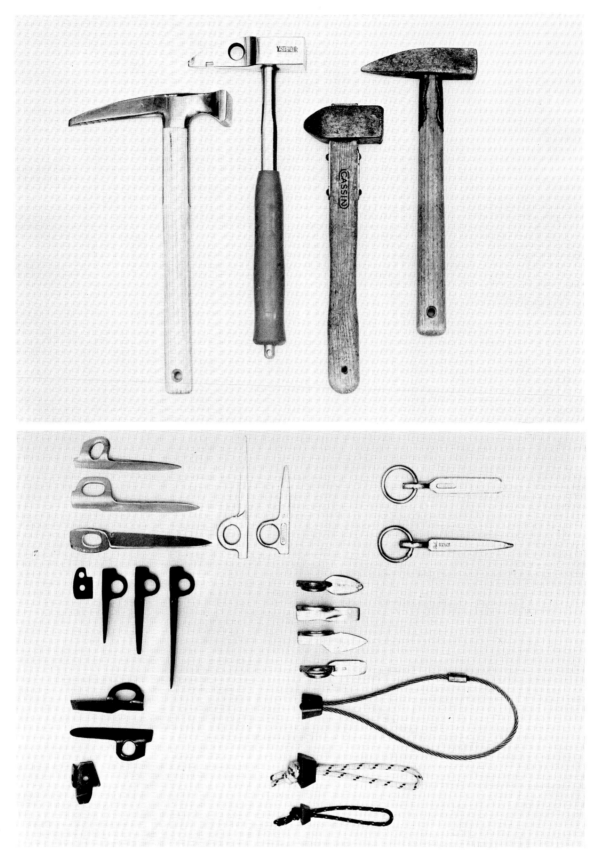

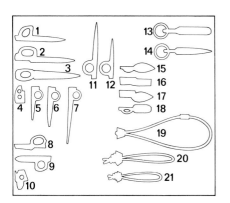

naturally without knots. Wood, despite its beauty, constitutes a weak point even in the case of a new ice-axe and all the more so in one which has seen several years' service. Sooner or later, wood will undoubtedly be replaced by some stronger and, above all, harder-wearing material; this has already been done in Scotland (the MacInnes ice-axe, the handle of which is of hiduminium).

The hallmark of a good ice-axe is first-class balance, so that it handles easily and the mountaineer uses it with maximum efficiency.

Length of the ice-axe. The usual length for an ice-axe is from 70 cm (28 ins) to 95 cm (38 ins), according to the height of the climber. Standing up, with the ice-axe held upright against his leg and the spike on the ground, he should be able to rest the palm of his hand on the head of the ice-axe.

Short ice-axes are used on steep ice climbs; being less cumbersome, they are also used on some rock climbs which include awkward stretches of ice (for example the Pilier Bonatti on the Drus).

Varieties of ice-axe. There are:

1. Standard ice-axes, made of ordinary steel, for climbers who will rarely or never have to cut steps.

2. Special ice-axes, which are lighter and made of stronger steel, with the result that the blade can be slenderer, terminating in an edge 5 cm (2 ins) wide.

3. Ice-axes which can be dismantled into two pieces. They are the same length as an ordinary ice-axe but can be taken apart into two pieces which stow easily in a rucksack; however, they are slightly heavier and even if they do not wobble they are inevitably less well balanced. The blade is of special steel.

Sword-knot. This prevents the novice from losing his ice-axe but is none the less an evasion, an easy way out, and is in fact inadvisable: it can cause an accident and, in the case of a fall, injuries. The mountaineer should school himself to hang on to his ice-axe until the habit becomes a conditioned reflex; he must learn to handle it neatly and be able to park it instantly between his rucksack and his back if he suddenly needs his hands free to climb a pitch of rock. All the same, on some long ice climbs, when the mountaineer needs his hands free from time to time, for example to put in ice-pitons, it is an advantage to have a sword-knot; this prevents all risk of losing the ice-axe, saves time, and cuts out the movements required to put the ice-axe between the back and rucksack, or hang it from the belt, either of which can sometimes be ticklish.

Carrying the ice-axe. In rock climbing, the ice-axe is stowed head downwards in the rucksack or hung on the back of it, in the loops provided for the purpose.

In a mixed climb, the best solution is to slip it between the back and the rucksack, when on rock; it can then be retrieved quickly on encountering ice.

On the approach march up to the hut I have often seen guides carrying their ice-axes between pack and back, not under one of the straps but lying on top of them; the ice-axe stays there by its own weight. I often use this method myself, in fact; it is the quickest one of all, as you can have the ice-axe in action at an instant's notice.

The thing that prolongs a climb and sometimes causes delay and danger is not slow climbing but the cumulative effect of tiresome little losses of time in handling the rope and changing over tools and equipment.

Maintenance. The point, the pick and the adze should be sharpened by grinding when they get blunted by use.

Hammer ice-axes

These are of two kinds, the first being more of an ice-axe than a hammer, the second more of a hammer than an ice-axe: (a) the short ice-axe with a hammer instead of the adze. With this, steps can be cut in ice, verglas removed if necessary, and pitons inserted; and (b) the hammer with a pointed peen. This is a hammer specially designed for ice. It is handier than the first kind and is particularly useful on very difficult verglassed rock, on which holds have to be cleared of verglas and pitons put in at frequent intervals.

Rock hammer

This should be fairly heavy, about 600 grammes (approximately 1 lb 6 oz), and the handle should be fairly long, for effective hitting. The head is of steel; one end is square, with a large striking face, the other pointed and fairly long. For unmixed rock climbing the point is short (as in the Cassin model, for example); in rock climbs where verglas is to be expected, perhaps with short stretches of ice as well, the point is longer (as in the models by Charlet, Simond and Chouinard).

Carrying the hammer. The hammer used to be attached to the wrist by a sword-knot but this is dangerous; the practice now is to hang it by a cord from the climber's belt. When not using the hammer the climber puts it into the hip pocket of his trousers or slips it into a sheath of cloth sewn vertically along the outer side of the trouser leg. But the hammer tends to slip out whenever he flexes the hip-joint. So the best answer is a sheath of leather or plastic hooked on to the shoulder-harness, in which the hammer rides head upwards.

Rock pitons

The use of pitons, like that of crampons, has come to stay; it is part of the technique of mountaineering. Still, one must try not to overdo it. When climbing the Arête Ryan on the Aiguille du Plan, or the Grépon Mer de Glace, it is no bad thing to remember that Franz Lochmatter and Peter Knubel made the first ascents of these in nailed boots and without pitons.

Pitons consist of a shank or blade, and a head with a hole to take a snap-link. They are made of mild steel, high-carbon steel or chrome molybdenum alloy steel, and are forged in one piece, the hole being punched out at the same time.

Some American and Russian pitons are made of light non-ferrous alloy, like many aircraft parts. This is doubtless a pointer to the future, the chief drawback of the present-day steel pitons being their weight.

Pitons vary widely, both in shape and in hardness.

Shape. At one time, pitons were *vertical* (with the hole continuing the line of the blade), or *horizontal* (with the direction of the hole at right-angles to the axis of the blade), the first being used in vertical cracks and the second in horizontal or oblique cracks; or *ring-pitons*, used especially in the Dolomites for abseils and pendulums. Nowadays the horizontal pitons are almost the only ones made, it having been found in practice that they are effective on nearly all occasions. But vertical pitons are still manufactured for use in rounded cracks, and also for the holes which occur particularly in limestone. The awkward thing about a piton being its weight (some climbs require an arsenal of fifty pitons weighing 8 lb or more, to which must be

Pitons, used in artificial climbing, are also important in free climbing, for belaying; as here, for example, in the direct route up the south face of the Cougourde.

44

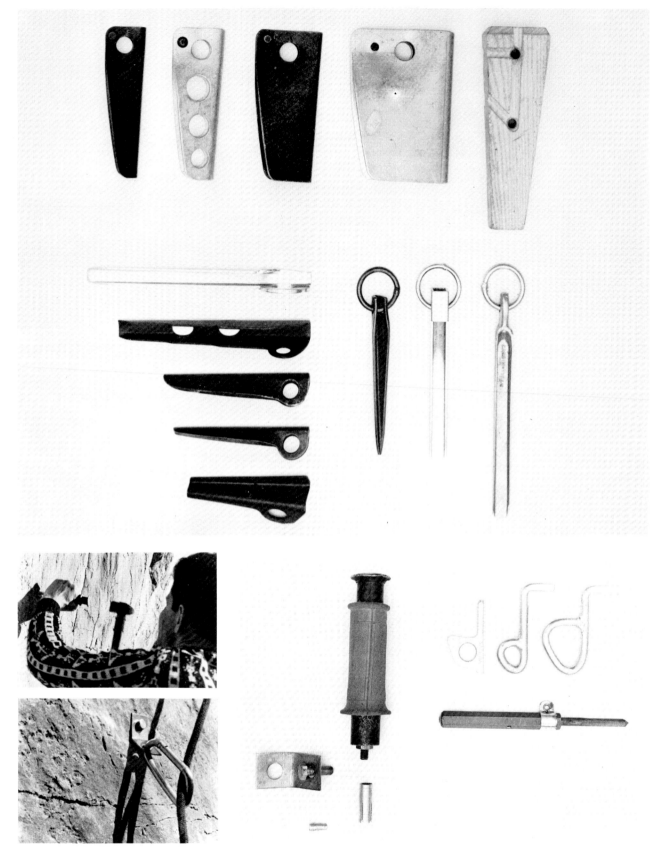

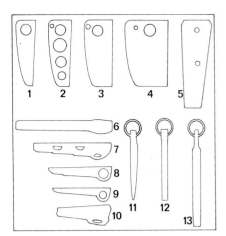

1. Chouinard angle-iron piton
2. Chouinard Bong-Bong
3. Chouinard angle-iron piton
4. Chouinard angle-iron piton
5. Wooden wedge
6. Simond angle-iron piton
7. Charlet angle-iron piton (with three positions for snap-link)
8. Chouinard angle-iron piton
9. Chouinard angle-iron piton
10. Leeper Z-section piton
11. Salewa ring piton
12. Charlet ring piton
13. Cassin ring piton

1. Drill for tubular gollot
   1a. Handle, with threaded tip which is screwed into the gollot for drilling
   1b. Tubular gollot with serrated end
   1c. Wedge
   1d. Plate, and screw which takes the place of the threaded tip of the handle after drilling has been completed, the wedge has been inserted in the serrated end of the gollot, and the gollot has been fixed in position.
2. Ordinary drill
3. Horizontal expansion bolt
4, 5. Vertical expansion bolt

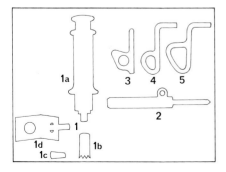

added the weight of the snap-links, rings, stirrups, hammer etc.), Simond produced the pioneer invention, rapidly copied by others, of pitons made of angle-iron or U-section, which are much lighter than solid pitons of the same size. These new pitons were intended for wide cracks; wooden wedges continued to be used for very wide ones. But since then Yvon Chouinard, designer of American pitons, has brought out V-section pitons ranging from the smallest size to the 'Bongs' which are even bigger than the wedges.

Flat pitons. According to size, pitons are classified as *supporting pitons,* the function of which is to permit progression (they need only support the climber's weight and have a very limited capacity to check a fall), and *safety pitons,* which can take a load of 1,500–2,000 kilos (only a little under $1\frac{1}{2}$–2 tons).

The smallest piton of all is the 'Rurp' (Realized Ultimate Reality Piton), the razor-blade piton manufactured by Chouinard. This is 1 cm long and 2·5 cm wide and is intended for cracks which are so slight as to be almost imperceptible; it can almost be said that it is the piton itself, made of extra-hard steel, which creates the crack into which it is forced; the ideal place to insert it is just where a crack starts. A strap from 4 to 6 cm long is used with this piton, either threaded through one of the two holes or secured round the piton, depending on the position in which the Rurp has been driven home.

Charlet has recently brought out his mini-piton, which is almost as small as the Rurp.

Chouinard also makes the extra-thin 'Knifeblade' piton, which comes in four sizes. Other very thin pitons, from 2·5 to 4 mm thick, are made by Charlet and by Simond; those made by Charlet have the eye offset so that the snap-link is as close to the rock as possible when the piton is in place.

All these thin, short pitons are made of chrome molybdenum steel.

Other flat-bladed pitons are altogether bigger, meant for driving deeper into the crack, and are designed for checking a fall; whatever their origin, French, Italian, Austrian or American, these are the traditional pitons; their mode of use, a function of their hardness, depends on the nature of the terrain. The direction of the eye is usually at right-angles to the plane of the blade but is in some cases at a different angle to it, the head of the piton having been slightly rotated (as in the Charlet Universel).

Angle-iron (etc.) pitons. These are used in wide cracks. If made in Europe (Simon, Charlet, Cassin, Stubaï) they are of U-section, or, rather, channel section (i.e. the section is right-angled), with nearly-parallel edges; a variant is the 'multi-hold' piton invented by Charlet, allowing three different positions of the snap-link or strap. The American pitons by Chouinard, and some of the Austrian pitons, are of V-section and have a slightly conical profile. The Leeper pitons are of Z-section.

European angle-iron pitons are never more than 12 mm thick. Charlet, on the other hand, makes a series which starts with angle-pitons and goes on up through the range of 'Bongs', the biggest of which are over 10 cm (4 ins) wide: bigger than wooden wedges.

Hardness. The hardness of a piton naturally depends on the steel or alloy of which it is made and the treatment given to the material during manufacture. Broadly speaking, and oversimplifying a little, it can be said that mild steel pitons mould themselves to the shape of the crack they are driven into; they lock into it, are often difficult to take out again and may emerge decidedly mangled. Contrariwise,

47

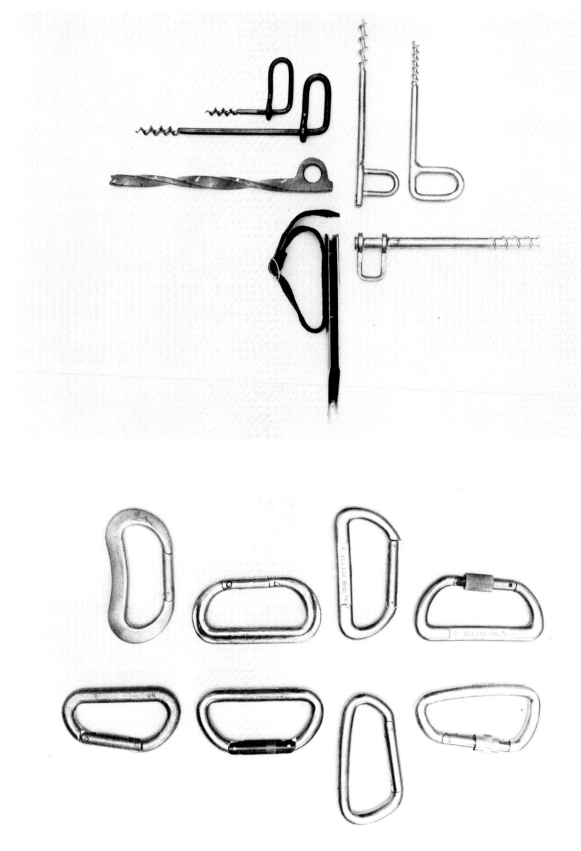

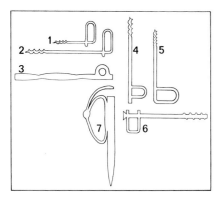

1. Stubaï ice-piton
2. Stubaï ice-piton
3. Salewa ice-piton
4. Charlet ice-piton
5. Salewa ice-piton
6. Salewa tubular ice-piton
7. Ice-dagger (U-section piton with hand-grip)

1. Kamet snap-link
2. Salewa snap-link
3. Allain snap-link
4. Allain snap-link with threaded safety device
5. Chouinard snap-link
6. Bonatti-Cassin snap-link
7. Simond snap-link
8. Simond snap-link with threaded safety device

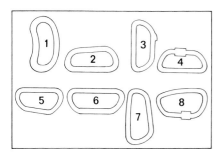

the rigid, extra-hard pitons of chrome molybdenum steel do not adapt themselves to the internal shape of the crack and do not lock into it, but become wedged–a different principle. If the spot where a hard piton is to be inserted is chosen carefully, both insertion and recovery are easy.

The two categories of piton are equally useful: the choice of one or the other depends on the characteristics of the rock being climbed. Comparatively soft pitons, such as those made by Cassin, are specially suitable for relatively soft rock (limestone or schist); ultra-hard pitons, which might break up the sides of the winding cracks found in soft rock, are suited to hard varieties of rock. Intermediate between the two extremes are the Simond and Charlet pitons, used all over the Western Alps.

Wooden wedges. Made of ash wood, these are in the shape of a truncated pyramid and have holes and grooves to accommodate a line.

Expansion bolts. These are small pitons, driven forcibly into a hole previously drilled in the rock. There are various kinds; most of them are of square-section (about 7 mm) bored in the rock. The drill consists of a handle and a steel shank. The latest kind of expansion bolt is a tubular sleeve with a serrated cutting end; this obviates the need for a drill.

Wedges. These, which are specially favoured by British mountaineers, and which work on the principle of a block stuck in a crack, are very effective provided they are competently used. The wedges– of steel or plastic–are of different sizes and shapes to suit different cracks.

Ice-pitons

The old-fashioned ice-pitons (bladed, tubular or channel) which were driven in with the hammer, have been replaced by ice-pitons which screw in and are a great improvement. They are something like corkscrews and are of two types: (a) slender solid screws (make a hole with the ice-axe to give the screw a start; do not hit with the hammer); (b) tubular screws (i.e. hollow, but threaded externally).

These screws have proved extremely beneficial to ice climbing, but even more so to belaying and roping down.

Ice-dagger. This is a point or hand-pick which is held in the free hand (the one not occupied with the ice-axe) and which helps to maintain balance when using the toe-spikes of crampons to climb a very steep ice slope.

Snap-links

These come in two sizes: standard and small.

Small snap-links can be used for attaching an étrier, rucksack or hammer, or for securing a piton while it is being taken out, but never for belaying. They are made of steel and are as heavy (65 gr or 2½ oz) as a standard snap-link in light alloy; the latter is decidedly preferable, the best answer in almost every case.

Standard size snap-links are used in all sorts of manoeuvres, and in belaying. They are made of steel or light alloy, in various shapes and thicknesses. Generally speaking, snap-links of light alloy, commonly known as Dural, are now as strong as the steel ones, with a

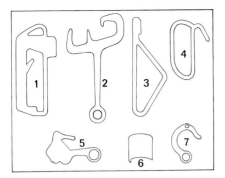

1. Jumar grip
2. Allain descendeur
3. Salewa Griff Fiffi
4. Asmu Griff Fiffi
5. Salewa-Hiebeler device
6. Magnone descendeur
7. Salewa Fiffi

breaking strain of between 1,800 and 2,500 kilos (3,970 lb and 5,511 lb) for a closed snap-link in either material. But their respective weights may vary by as much as 50 or 100 per cent, according to the types chosen for comparison: a snap-link in light alloy may weigh from 65 to 80 gr (from $2\frac{1}{2}$ oz to a little less than 3 oz) as against 130 to 135 gr (nearly 5 oz) for steel. Experiments with an open snap-link show that the breaking strain is diminished in most cases by at least a third; like ropes, snap-links are being carefully studied by the U.I.A.A. At the present time the ASMU snap-link in chrome vanadium steel is the strongest, with a breaking strain of 3,800 kilos (7,875 lb) when closed but only about two-fifths of that amount when open. Of course a snap-link is meant to be closed and has a spring to keep it closed, but in a fall it may – if not hooked on properly, or if it hits a knob or sharp edge of rock – come open or half open. Some snap-links, both in steel and Dural, have a threaded portion, and a threaded sleeve which screws over it, to keep them closed; these, sometimes called safety snap-links, are used for belaying and sometimes for roping up, but not for progression.

Again, a snap-link is intended to support a vertically applied load. But in the event of a fall it is possible for the ropes to move in such a way that the strain bears momentarily from side to side of the link, instead of from end to end; and if the side to which this happens is the opening one, and even if this is closed, perhaps with a threaded sleeve for extra security, and even if the strain is only slight, the link can break.

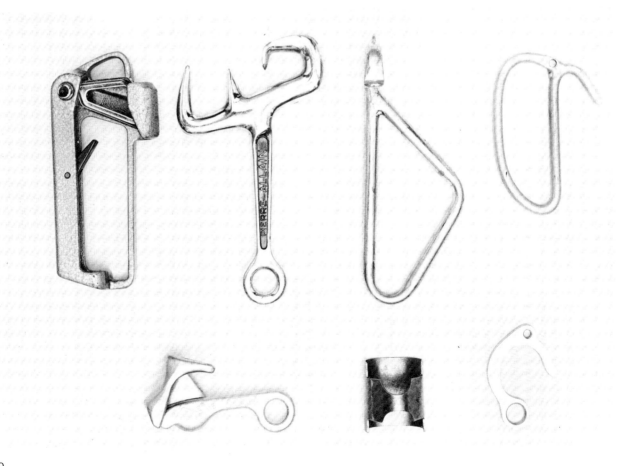

The best type of snap-link for use with étriers is the Allain which has no screw for keeping it shut. Other kinds are difficult to open or close as soon as the climber's weight comes on to the étrier to which the snap-link is fastened.

Finally, there seem to be obstacles to ensuring a steady flow of production and consistent quality, even in a single model of snap-link. Considerable improvements in this situation are no doubt to be expected, to the benefit of all concerned.

There is much variety in the shape of snap-links; they may be oval, pear-shaped, curved inwards on one side, a regular or distorted D, and so on. The latest Simond model is very conveniently shaped.

Descendeurs. These are small devices, made of light alloy in some cases, which permit fast roping down in all circumstances and avoid friction between the rope and the climber's body. The original inventor was Pierre Allain, to whom many improvements in mountaineering equipment are due; several other makers have since brought out their own models. Some descendeurs, the Magnone for example, are not so much an independent item of equipment as a small accessory for attaching to a snap-link. The Magnone descendeur consists of a small metal component weighing 100 gr (about $3\frac{1}{2}$ oz), in the form of a short, flattened roller which can be inserted into any standard size snap-link and acts as a brake on the abseiling rope; a second snap-link on the opposite side prevents the descendeur from jumping out and enables the braking action to be regulated.

Sticht-Salewa brake plate. A metal plate used in a certain version of the running belay technique.

Jumar. A mechanized Prusik knot, as it were, making it possible to go up, and even down, a hanging rope. It consists of a hand-grip embodying an automatic device which, when weight is applied, locks on to the rope; attached to the grip is an étrier.

A variation of the Jumar is the Salewa stirrup, which has no hand-grip; this reduces its weight by more than half but is otherwise a drawback.

Sticht-Salewa brake plate

Étriers (stirrups)

Étriers were originally made of line with loops in it; platforms (flat rungs) were subsequently added and the whole étrier, or set of stirrups, might have four, five or even six of these. The number was then reduced to two or three and has now settled down at three or four.

Length. This depends partly on the height of the mountaineer but still more on how supple he is in the legs, that is to say how good he is at raising his knees towards his chin; it also depends on the distance between the platforms and to some extent on their number, three or four. If we reckon that a climber can put in a piton not more than 220 cm (7 ft 4 ins) above the level of his feet, and that he is capable of a vertical stride of 70 cm (28 ins), the total length of the stirrup assembly will be 1 m 50 (5 ft) including snap-links, or 1 m 35 without snap-links. For a smaller individual the assembly will be of the same length, in view of the fact that the upper limit will be reduced by the same amount; for example, 200 cm–50 cm = 1 m 50.

Platforms. If these are too wide they are cumbersome and heavy; if too narrow they are difficult to get the foot into. A happy medium is when the internal distance between the two lines is from 12 to 15 cm (4·8 to 6 ins).

For belaying in artificial climbing, the nylon sling, Robbins model, is both light and very comfortable (1).

Yvon Chouinard climbing an ice wall: crampons with horizontal front points; ice-axe in right hand; left hand using an ice-piton (2).

The platforms are 'stopped' (prevented from slipping down) by a plain knot, or, better, a figure-eight knot, below the platform; there is no knot above.

It is a good thing for the distance between platforms to be progressively smaller as they go up. For a four-platform assembly, 135 cm (4 ft 6 ins) long excluding snap-links, a suggested spacing is 46, 38, 30, 32 cm (18½, 15, 12, 12¾ ins); for three platforms, 55, 45, 35 cm (22, 18, 14 ins).

The étrier can be suspended by means of an ordinary knotted loop, but even if it is very short this loop has the great disadvantage of narrowing the space for the foot to enter in making use of the top platform. It is better to fix the stirrup to the snap-link by a clove hitch (which is easier to undo in the event of one's wanting to use the étrier to climb up a rope with the help of a self-tightening knot); or else two loops can be made, one in each of the upper ends of the line. Below the bottom platform the two lines are knotted together, allowing a second étrier to be hooked on if required.

Étriers can also be made out of stiff webbing without platforms, the method used in California. This is a variation of the earliest method of all, with webbing replacing line. The advantages are: (a) the webbing is broad; (b) the foot is securely held, and if you want to sit down the webbing is comparatively supple and more comfortable than a platform; (c) given the strength of the webbing (breaking strain 1,900 kilos, about 4,190 lb), the étrier, and in particular the loop at the top, can be used for belaying; (d) webbing étriers get hung up less than those with platforms, and make no noise.

On the other hand, the feet do not as a rule slip into webbing étriers as easily as into those with platforms.

Fiffi. This is a plain hook (instead of the snap-link) at the top of the étrier, with a piece of line connecting the étrier to the climber, which you can pull behind you like a little dog (whence the name). In climbs where artificial aids are used a great deal the Fiffi saves an appreciable amount of time. Some climbers use the hook but not the line, which tends to get hung up and also impedes the movements of the legs.

Griff-Fiffi. This is an improved version of the Fiffi, with a hand-grip below the hook.

Swing (escarpolette). This is a wooden or plastic board, slung on line, on which one sits when belaying in artificial climbing. The board can be replaced to advantage by an oblong piece of nylon fabric, reinforced with, and slung by means of, webbing straps (the Robbins sling, made in the United States). The fabric-and-straps assembly is lighter, more comfortable and much less awkward than the rigid type.

Crampons

Crampons make it possible to move safely and enjoyably on steep hard snow and on ice. They are made of special steel so as to be strong yet light (about 500 to 600 gr, between 1 lb 2 oz and 1 lb 6 oz), whatever the type: adjustable or non-adjustable, short thin points or comparatively broad and high, ten points in all or twelve.

Since crampons are items which have to be absolutely trustworthy in steep, difficult places, the following points are essential:

1. The crampons must fit the boots perfectly. It is worth pointing out once again that in all mountaineering equipment, including crampons, approximations simply will not do. A crampon which

1

shifts slightly under the foot is capable, despite being strapped to the boot, of causing a serious accident. A well-adjusted crampon should lightly grip the sole of the boot, so that it would tend to stay on even without straps; when weight is brought to bear on the crampon it should wedge itself tighter on the boot and not 'float' at all, even fractionally. The crampons should be adjusted to the boots not with brute force and ignorance and a hammer, but by gradually screwing them tight, and the points should be exactly below the border of the sole. Finally, remember when putting on crampons – which sometimes has to be done in pitch darkness – that there are such things as a right crampon and a left crampon!

2. The points must always be sharp. It is true that on snow, even hard snow, slightly blunted points go in nicely, but on ice they do not bite at all. In 1956, coming down Mont Blanc by the normal route, a rope of climbers whose crampons were blunt but still sharp enough for snow, were caught unawares and 'took off' when they were at the level of the Mauvaise Arête and had a short steep patch of hard smooth ice to cross; they fell as far as the Grand Plateau.

3. The straps, no matter which of the various arrangements of them is used, must be in good condition, and neither too long nor too short.

4. Finally, an acute danger which must always be forestalled is that, in certain conditions of snow, and especially when passing from one condition to another condition and temperature of the snow, the snow sticks to the bottoms of the crampons and forms a ball between the points. The broader and longer the points, the more liable they are to clog in this manner.

Oversimplifying considerably, we can divide crampons into two kinds, according to the going: those with long, fairly wide points for snow, even very hard snow; and those with short, fine points for ice.

Short fine points do not go deep enough into snow and provide poor security when traversing; conversely, long broad points are useless and even a handicap on ice – because, penetrating only a fraction of an inch, they act as miniature stilts and also introduce unwanted leverage.

On comparatively easy climbs ten-point crampons are sufficient, but on any climb involving steep slopes it is much better to use the twelve-point kind; these have ten vertical points and two in front which are almost horizontal, pointing slightly downwards. It was Laurent Grivel, a guide and blacksmith of Courmayeur, who in 1931 displayed his outstanding common sense and intelligence by inventing the twelve-point crampon, the leading points of which enable the climber to make a direct ascent even on a very steep slope. In some crampons the two leading points are almost vertical and are too close to the first fully vertical ones; this is wrong and should be avoided.

Indeed, the first two vertical points need not be exactly vertical but can advantageously be inclined forward a little, so as to relieve the two leading points of part of the load, which is the whole weight of the body.

Finally, there are crampons with only ten points but with the two front ones horizontal, in other words eight vertical points plus two almost horizontal ones in front. They are excellent for mixed climbing, and at 450 gr (16 oz) the Grivel ten-point (eight plus two) crampons are the lightest of all. Personally, I have had a pair of them since 1946 and the climbs I have made with them include the ascent of the north face of the Matterhorn, in 1949, on which they were absolutely satisfactory.

2

Most crampons are articulated; but on long, difficult ice climbs some people prefer rigid, unarticulated crampons.

An important feature is that the crampons should not shift at all when, on a steep ice slope, the climber does not so much put his feet down as kick his toes into the slope so as to get a good hold with the leading points. In order to give the necessary firmness, the main body of the crampon should be as nearly as possible in line with the leading points.

Crampons with ten or twelve points, whether long or short, may be of either the adjustable or non-adjusting type. Some crampons can be adjusted for both length and breadth, others only for length or only for breadth. Though adjustable crampons have the advantage that they can be fitted to boots of different sizes, they have the disadvantages of being heavier, not quite so strong and comparatively complicated, and it can be very annoying if, for example when negotiating rocks during a mixed climb, screw-threads or a nut or wire get damaged. In principle, and in a shop, adjustable crampons are ideal; but in practice, in difficult conditions, they may be the reverse.

Ascent of Mont Blanc by the Arête des Bosses; right background, the Aiguille de Bionnassay.

Ascent of Mont Maudit by the Arête de la Tour Ronde.

Methods of fastening. A long strap, about 5 ft 6 ins, is still the best method so far devised for fixing the crampon to the boot. It has the drawback of being a little slow to put on, but it is worth sacrificing four or five minutes of the day if the result is that the crampons are really secure and firm. The strap is put on criss-cross round the foot and fastened with a non-slip metal buckle; it can be of hemp, leather or nylon. The advantage of nylon is that neither humidity nor low temperatures cause it to shrink, so that the risk of frostbite is reduced; but it does often tend to slip gradually through the buckles.

There are also methods using short fixed straps of hemp, leather or nylon combined with portions of rubber; these make the crampons quick to put on, but they weigh more and are apt to be less firm.

When crampons are not in use they are carried on top of the rucksack. Some rucksacks have strings and a protective plate for carrying crampons, but guides prefer to put them on top of the rucksack. If properly stowed they do no harm to the mountaineer or his outfit, and do not wobble about; and, as always, the nearer the weight is to the back the easier it is to carry.

Crampons with horizontal leading points make it possible to climb steep ice-faces. It is interesting to note that the mountaineer's position on ice is similar to that adopted on a rock-face of comparable steepness.

Roping

The best way of roping up is by means of a shoulder-harness, the requirements for which are the following:

1. The harness must be complete, that is to say it should consist of a belt, two shoulder-straps and two thigh-straps. It is possible to have all these straps adjustable but this makes the harness clumsy, heavier and more complicated, and is in any case unnecessary: the harness is a personal, individual piece of equipment, and if, instead of a snap-link being used to fasten it to the climbing rope, the rope is passed directly through the two loops of the harness, the belt can be tightened or let out to suit oneself.

Contrary to what might be feared, a complete shoulder-harness, if well designed, does not in any way hamper the climber's movements, even if he has frequently to straddle widely or bring a knee up very high. The complete shoulder-harness is particularly suitable for artificial climbing; it is even more serviceable in the event of a fall, especially if the victim is left hanging over a void, for example in a crevasse or below an overhang, because instead of being suspended by his waist or chest, as in the traditional methods of roping up, he can sit at ease in his harness and, having his hands free, can co-operate promptly and effectively in his own rescue.

2. The climbing rope must pass directly through the shoulder-straps of the harness (which, as already mentioned, allows the belt to be tightened or slackened at will); it must not be coupled to the harness by a snap-link. Certainly a snap-link makes a quick and easy fastening, but it is also highly dangerous and must be ruled right out. Even a snap-link with a screw safety device is dangerous in this context because, unfortunately, any snap-link may easily break under the sudden heavy strain of a fall; in fact even an ordinary pull can break it if the strain comes across the link, i.e. laterally, and on the side that opens. This drawback can be mitigated by laying up two links together, with the movable parts on opposite sides; but in addition to being heavy and cumbersome this arrangement largely cancels out the advantage of quickness and convenience.

Moreover, in artificial climbing it is satisfying to be as close to the piton as possible; but, unlike roping up directly to the harness, the loop of the climbing rope which enters the snap-link, plus the link itself, robs the climber of some 4–8 ins of height below each piton.

Finally, since first-hand experience is more convincing than argument, here is part of an account by the great Swiss mountaineer, Michel Vaucher, in *Les Alpes*, the journal of the Swiss Alpine Club:

'An observable fact, both in climbing schools and in the real thing, is that more and more climbers are roping up on to a belt or a shoulder-harness. In the event of a fall, the various straps of the harness distribute the shock to different parts of the body, a very desirable arrangement. But where people go wrong, both with the belt and with the harness, is that they fasten the rope directly to a snap-link, of the so-called safety type. The advantages of doing so, as against the conventional method, are: (a) the climber has less rope about him; and (b) roping up is quicker.

'But this practice of roping directly to a snap-link puts the climber profoundly at risk in the event of a fall. Safety snap-links with a breaking strain of anything up to 3,500 kilos (about 7,700 lb) are designed, like all snap-links, to function "straight", that is, with the load in line with their longitudinal axis.

What is suspended on the ropes is not the climber himself but the harness in which he is sitting; an important distinction, both in the case of a fall and in artificial climbing. It is essential that the harness provide overall support; its purchase must not be concentrated on the upper part of the body alone.

'But what happens when the link is connected to a harness?

'The link is under strain in line with the body, and the climbing rope bears on the weakest part of the link, and across the link, not along it. Thus loaded, these very same snap-links sometimes give way under a strain of less than 200 kilos (440 lb). A fatal accident (which took place this year) and a fall (of which I was an eye-witness) were both caused by this method of roping up. With my own eyes I once saw a friend of mine fall – he was No. 2 on the rope; the snap-link broke while he was simply hanging in the air. There was no sudden impact, just a steady strain of under 90 kilos (200 lb). His fall was not serious, as we were only 9 feet above the ground at the time, but I shuddered at the thought that my friend had been using this method for the previous two years.

'If the leader falls the impact on the rope is high. But the manufacturers have been at pains to provide astonishingly strong ropes, able to withstand falls from over 90 feet. So it is very silly to interpose dubious connecting devices and thus undermine the magnificent safety offered by the rope.'

Personally, I do not use a snap-link but slip the rope directly through the two shoulder-straps of the harness; in other words, I rope up the harness itself (using a bowline knot for the purpose).

In artificial climbing, the bowline loop by which the rope is attached to the harness should be as short as possible, so that the climber under traction should lose as little height as possible; this enables him to climb overhangs – such as the Toit de Sarre, nearly 100 feet of downward-sloping overhang – without excessive fatigue.

There are various methods of roping up without using a shoulder-harness. On the one hand, there are methods which are partial approximations to the harness, such as the rope sling, or the use of a length of rope (about 8 metres, or 26 feet, of hemp rope) which is passed at least seven times round the trunk; either of these can be so arranged as to include braces (shoulder-straps). In both cases it is a common habit to use a snap-link to join the sling or rope to the climbing rope. In theory, the snap-link takes the strain the right way, along its length, the direction in which it is strongest; but in a fall, during which the strain may be exerted in various directions, all unforeseeable, there is nothing to prevent it from coming on the link in the wrong direction, where the link is weakest.

On the general principle that, in mountaineering, the best is just good enough, it seems to me that these hybrid methods are to be avoided and that the best way of roping up is the complete shoulder-harness.

There is also, of course, the classical method of roping up with the climbing rope itself, making (according to the knot employed) either a single loop round the waist or two loops, one round the waist and one over the shoulder. This method does not possess the advantages of the shoulder-harness, but it does avoid the drawbacks of a snap-link.

Before dealing with knots, we must discuss the place where the roping-up loop is fastened; the answer will apply equally to all methods of roping up. The traditional practice is to pass the loop through the belt, and for my part I have always had much respect for our early predecessors; everything they did had common sense behind it. But everyone, including them, can be wrong, and the present fashion is to rope up not at the level of the waist but the chest, under the armpits; at any rate this is the technique used in Austria and America. The aim is to situate the point of attachment directly above the centre of gravity and to ensure that if the climber falls he will not go down head-first.

The coils of rope, carried over one shoulder and round the chest, should always be fastened in such a way that they stay together and cannot come loose. When needed again the whole rope can be quickly and easily lifted off in one piece.

I suggest we must start by remembering that nothing is ever perfect, and that we are faced with a choice between methods of which each has its own disadvantages.

The disadvantages of roping up to the waist are that, in a fall, the climber may be head-downwards, and that when the fall is suddenly and violently arrested the spine and floating ribs may be damaged.

The disadvantages of roping up to the chest are that, in a fall, the impact of the rope is taken both by the spinal column and by the rib-cage. After that there may be difficulty in breathing, the rib-cage being compressed by the rope which is supporting the climber hanging on the end of it; moreover the pectoral and dorsal muscles (which are quite as important in pulling as the arm muscles) are under pressure from the rope and are not easy to bring into action; and finally, the worst disadvantage of all is that if the climber is very supple–which women, in particular, often are–he or she may slip right out of the loop, even if it is provided with braces and has also been done up as tightly as possible round the chest, which in any case is uncomfortable.

As a result of questioning numerous climbers, guides and members of rescue teams I find that, at any rate on the Mont Blanc massif, they have neither witnessed, nor discovered by investigation after the event, falls in which the body descended head-first in consequence of a seesaw movement imparted when the fall was checked by the rope, a movement which would be imputable to the fact that the head is the heaviest part of the body. (This does not mean, of course, that no one has ever fallen head-first; but in those cases the fall was head-first from the start). For my own part, if there is no harness I prefer to rope up at waist level or perhaps slightly higher, but in any case not under the armpits, round the chest. Presumably things are different in the Eastern Alps, seeing that both the Austrian and German Alpine Clubs recommend roping up at chest level; perhaps the reason is that the rock walls in the Eastern Alps, mostly limestone, are generally more vertical than the granite walls of the Western Alps.

There is a fairly comfortable way of roping up for artificial climbing which can be used if one has no harness. Do not simply pass the two climbing ropes round the waist but through the belt-loops of the trousers (these loops are elongated, tubular-fashion, on some trousers). The advantage is double: the fabric of the trousers protects the climber from the rope; and directly the climber is in traction on the pitons he is supported by his trousers and more or less sitting in them. We were using this method in the Calanques thirty years ago.

Knots for roping up

Bowline. Whether a shoulder-harness is used, or whether roping up is executed with the climbing rope itself, the best knot, in my estimation, is the bowline. (In the first case, the climbing rope is passed through the two loops on the belt of the harness and made into a small loop secured by a bowline; in the second, a larger loop is made, round the waist, and similarly secured by a bowline.)

The bowline can be single, double or even triple. Although very reliable, it is easy to undo, even after weight has been placed on the rope. When making a bowline, always pull it tight and back it up with a stop-knot in case the slipperiness of the nylon makes it start coming open.

Overhand knot (simple knot, plain knot). Easy and quick to tie, and holds well; but not recommended, being hard to untie as soon as weight has been brought to bear on the rope.

Figure-eight knot (derived from the figure-eight stop-knot). Also useful for making the loops in a rope ladder.

Fisherman's knot. Suitable for two climbers, one at each end of the rope; but absolutely 'out' in an intermediate position, when there are more than two climbers on the rope, as its two halves can then start slipping.

Guide's knot.

Chair knot, single or double.

Stop-knots

The purpose of a stop-knot is to prevent a rope from passing a certain point, for example in fixing the rungs when making an étrier, or for temporarily stopping the end of a rope which has started to fray.

Overhand knot. Difficult to undo once it has been pulled tight.

Figure-eight knot.

'Capucin' knot, with an odd number of crossings.

Knots for joining two ropes of equal thickness

Overhand knot. Hard to undo.

Figure-eight knot.

Fisherman's knot. Excellent.

Reef knot. Suitable if the rope is against a surface, not hanging free. Take care that both free ends are on the same side of the standing parts, and that they lie flat along the standing parts (otherwise the result will be a thief knot or granny, both of which are unsafe).

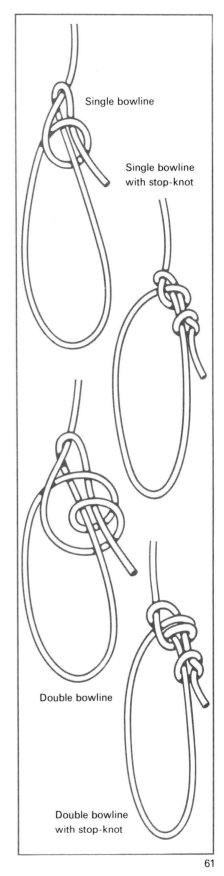

Single bowline

Single bowline with stop-knot

Double bowline

Double bowline with stop-knot

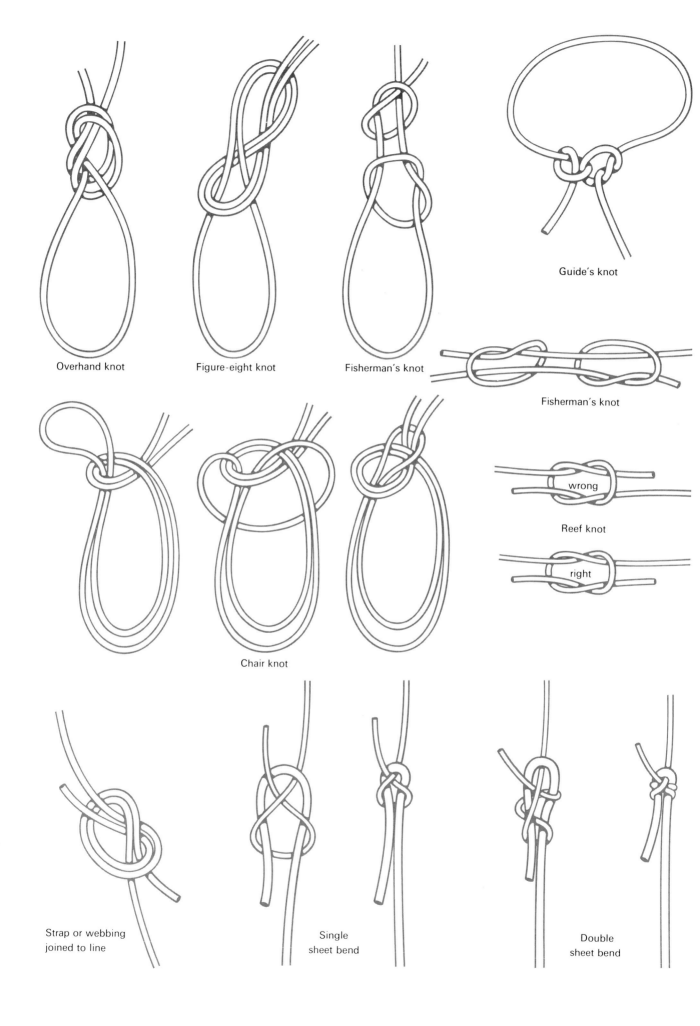

Overhand knot

Figure-eight knot

Fisherman's knot

Guide's knot

Fisherman's knot

wrong

Reef knot

right

Chair knot

Strap or webbing
joined to line

Single
sheet bend

Double
sheet bend

Knot for joining two ropes of different thicknesses

Sheet bend. The plain loop, without a crossing, is made in the thicker rope; the half-hitch, or loop with crossing, in the thinner. If the latter loop is made once only, the result is a single sheet bend; if twice, a double sheet bend.

Self-tightening knots

These are very useful knots, especially in the case of a fall, when they are valuable both to the man belaying and to the man belayed. In abseiling, they provide for self-belaying.

Prusik knot. At once the principal knot of this class, and the simplest. The greater the difference between the thickness of the rope and that of the line sling attached to it, the better the Prusik knot holds. The line can be wound four, six or eight times round the rope; the turns forming each of the two spirals are made from the middle towards the outside, and the two must evenly match each other.

Alpenverein knot. This too was devised by Dr Prusik. It can be used for two ropes of the same thickness. It is not so easy to undo as the Prusik knot.

Self-tightening knot on snap-link. Slip a line sling into a snap-link, then wind doubled line spirally round the entire length of the non-opening side of the link. The advantage of this self-blocking knot is the ease with which it can be slid along the rope when required.

Machard knot. Take a piece of nylon rope about 120 cm (4 ft) long and 8 or 9 mm (about $\frac{13}{16}''$) thick; double it; wind it three times spirally round the climbing rope, with the loop (the closed end) at the top; join the other ends together with an overhand knot and either pass the loop so formed through the upper loop, or join the two with a snap-link.

Clove hitch. This is better than a 'queue de vache' for belaying to a snap-link, in a relay; and is useful when using a fixed rope as a handrail. (A 'queue de vache' – literally 'cow's tail' – is a fixed loop made in a rope by means of an appropriate knot.) Special advantages of the clove hitch are that it can be made with one hand; that its position is easy to vary; and that whereas with the 'queue de vache' the rope must be taken out of the snap-link in order to tie the knot, with the clove hitch this is unnecessary.

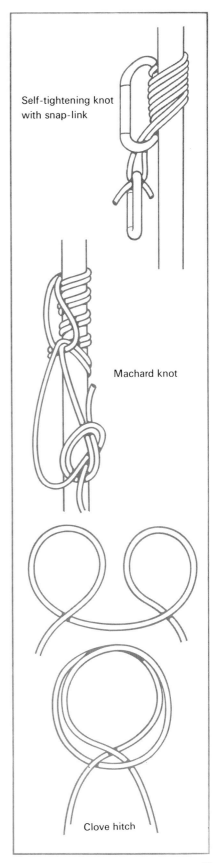

Self-tightening knot with snap-link

Machard knot

Clove hitch

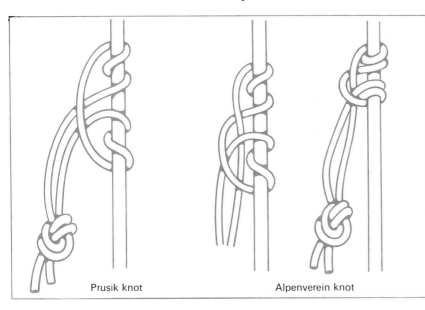

Prusik knot   Alpenverein knot

Technique and balance

Snow, ice and rock constitute a world which, if not hostile, is at any rate indifferent. Nevertheless, anyone who comes to love that world – with a love which is always unique and free, always peculiar to the individual – is confronted by interesting problems: exactly which route to pick, and the actions and movements required to follow it successfully to its climax, the arrival at the summit. Snow, ice and rock thus become companions who keep framing questions, companions to whom the mountaineer must make reply; climbing is an uninterrupted dialogue, a series of close exchanges between two partners whose essence is reciprocal; so that the world of snow, ice and rock becomes a friendly thing, part of ourselves. A crack, an overhang, a block jutting out from a sérac, are questions; the answers are contributed by technique, whose ingredients are love, instinct and conscious thought. This is why there is one way of utilizing a hold if it is well defined, and another if it is slight and superficial; and a certain manner of pulling oneself up on an étrier; and why crampons are used differently according to whether the slope is almost vertical or less sharply inclined. But there is one fundamental sensation which is always there, permeating this multiplicity of details, positions, situations and movements: the sensation of being in equilibrium – the sense of balance and the conscious cultivation of it.

In the whole proposition of climbing, so to speak, it seems to me that the first term to enunciate is this state of balance. Yet I hardly ever heard the word 'balance' when I was a trainee guide, hardly ever used it myself after I had become an instructor, and have hardly ever read it in manuals on climbing, even outstandingly good ones apart from this omission. Movements are described but there is no mention of balance: the balance of a bird on a branch; balance which enables you to climb easily, even in artificial climbing, which has the reputation of being difficult and tiring. Whereas most sports – particularly skiing – have movement-at-speed as their keynote and are therefore dynamic, in mountaineering the accelerations are so slight as to be a negligible quantity, and in consequence the climber's movements are a virtually unbroken succession of positions of equilibrium.

This is not a book on the most advanced forms of climbing; there are others which deal with the latest, most sophisticated technical developments. Curiously, however, even these make little or no mention of balance, the factor which, if properly used, eliminates useless and frustrating expenditure of energy. I have known expert climbers with a natural sense of balance and it was a pleasure to watch them climbing; everything looked easy. Gino Soldà is one of these. Others had apparently acquired a sense of balance by sheer dogged effort; they were equally successful but less pleasing to the eye, their style had remained jerky and staccato. And there were others who had never acquired it at all, despite years of practice. It is interesting to note, by the way, that limestone climbers almost always possess it but that it is comparatively rare among granite climbers. One very experienced climber of my acquaintance successfully carried out a number of really big climbs, but always laboriously. He had a complete command of technique, yet climbed badly. Perhaps no one had ever mentioned balance to him; perhaps he had never observed and analysed it in others, and deliberately, experimentally, tested it

Whenever the rock-face is slightly less than vertical it is a good thing to remind yourself that it is perfectly possible for your feet to support you on their own, with the hands not touching the rock. This makes you realize that most of the work is done by the feet; the hands merely accompany the movement.

Whenever possible, climb in the same way as you would climb a ladder.

Free climbing consists of a succession of two alternating phases: first the climber leans outward from the rock-face so as to get a good view of the handholds above his head and the footholds at knee and waist level, and to plan the next stage in his advance; second, he comes close to the rock again and carries out the moves thus prepared.

in himself. The result was that he gave a misleading impression of strength and came close to falling on more than one occasion; and on limestone, where he was never at ease, he was like a snared bird, or a bird with four feet instead of two. The truth is that a rock slab or an ice slope—like so many other things in life—can be tackled in more than one way; if we assume (to render comparison possible) that a given pitch is to be tackled along certain lines, technically speaking, there will still be two ways of climbing it, and the difference between them is a trifle, yet all-important: the difference between keeping the weight vertically above the feet and letting it come out of the vertical; and between having the legs bent or rigidly straight when there has to be a rocking movement, with the knees swinging forward.

Of course there are some strenuous pitches—slanting cracks, for example, or a place that has to be climbed on the layback—where the whole weight of the body is inclined outwards; but even in this kind of climbing a given series of movements can be harsh and jerky, or supple and smooth, according to the degree of co-ordination and rhythm between them.

What has to be remembered is the very obvious fact that the act of climbing consists of raising the body, moving it upwards, and subsequently moving it down. Hence the best way of resisting the force of gravity (which means, in fact, getting to the top in safety and with enjoyment, and not allowing fatigue to jeopardize either of these) is to make the legs and feet support the weight of the body whenever possible; the function of the hands and arms is simply to help in keeping the torso vertical, so that its weight bears directly on the pelvic girdle and from thence to the feet.

A fireman going up a tall ladder, even if the ladder is practically vertical, does not haul himself up from rung to rung with his hands but supports himself on his feet, stepping from rung to rung and using his hands merely for additional support.

If a pole is standing vertically its whole weight bears on its base, and little or no force is required to keep it upright. But if it is out of the vertical the case is altered: you must grasp it firmly in your hand instead of merely propping it with two fingers. Conversely, the more nearly vertical it is, the more directly its weight comes on to the bottom end and the less prone the end is to slide along the ground.

The word 'climbing' automatically evokes a mental picture of someone hanging on by his hands, and perhaps even only by them. But it would be more expedient, and in fact truer, to think of climbing as the act of walking on sloping ground which at times approximates to the vertical. We walk on flat ground; we also walk upstairs. A rock-face is a staircase, and it requires no great stretch of the imagination to think of a staircase with very narrow treads. Because contemporary climbing boots have extremely rigid soles, thanks to the metal plate which forms the middle layer of the sole, the climber has only to get a toe-hold on a 'tread' of the 'staircase' to be securely supported without putting much strain on the arms.

From such a hold he is enabled by flexion and extension of the knee – an essential item of technique which must be learnt and, above all, learnt consciously – to go on climbing: that is, to stand upright on the leading foot, without needing extra holds, or specially deep ones, for his hands. Only when the 'treads' of the 'staircase' have become very slight and shallow, or when the 'risers' are so many overhangs, so that the general angle of the 'stairs' approaches or even exceeds the vertical, does the climber really need handholds, not just to pull himself up by but to hold his body slightly away from the rock, while his weight continues to be supported as much as possible by his legs and feet. He will notice, moreover, that the more weight he puts on his feet the better they grip, and that the shallower the footholds the truer does this become.

In practice, situations like this do not often occur; in the mountains, especially in the Western Alps, there are plenty of fairly steep faces but very few genuine verticals or overhangs.

However, even on a not particularly steep face the beginner is naturally attracted by handholds; he soon starts clutching them and indeed using them not just to stay in position but to suspend his weight, with the result that he gets tired, then frightened, then paralysed. He holds on desperately, often with his arms at full stretch, as if clutching a lifebuoy, in places where he could be standing perfectly balanced on his feet if only he had studied the footholds in advance, simultaneously reminding himself that climbing simply consists of walking, with the knees being raised a little higher than usual.

In fact, the successive operations in climbing can be reduced, at the cost of a little oversimplification, to the following:

1. The climber pauses and takes stock, perhaps even leaning away from the rock-face a little to get a good look at the handholds and footholds above him.

The body-weight is resting entirely on the feet, which are level with each other; it is wholly in their keeping except when the climber puts a gap between the rock-face and himself in order to detect and study

the holds he is going to use next; while doing this he uses his hands and arms to hold his trunk in position and prevent himself from falling backwards, with the result that they are under slight tension.

2. Having made his inspection he now raises one foot; by flexion at hip and knee he places the toes of what becomes the uphill foot in the hold he has picked; in some cases he will raise a hand and arm as well.

At this point he has the choice of two methods of bringing up his body-weight so as to stand upright on the uphill foot. He can either:

3. Pull with his arms – making them take almost the whole of his weight until he is able to transfer it to the uphill foot and leg; in which case the foot and leg will merely have accompanied the movement. Or, alternatively, he can use the leg and foot to do the work, in two moves, of which the first flows smoothly into the second, thus:

First, transfer the body-weight from the downhill foot to the uphill one, the uphill leg being bent at hip and thigh. This transfer necessitates swinging the uphill knee forwards or sideways: forwards if the rock-face is not too steep; sideways if it is. Directly on making this movement with the knee the climber experiences definitely and precisely the sensation of having transferred his weight from the downhill to the uphill foot; to express it in still closer detail, the 80 kilos (176 lb) of his weight was previously on the downhill foot and is now on the uphill one, the knee and hip of which are bent.

Second, he extends (straightens) the uphill knee and thigh so as to bring his body standing upright on the uphill foot.

During these two moves, all that the hands and arms have done is to accompany and guide the transfer of weight and the subsequent extension of knee and hip.

In the first of the two methods, the effort, load and fatigue are assumed by the arms; in the second, by the legs.

Nine times out of ten, when you hear people say of a beginner 'He's improving fast, he's really promising', the reason is not that he has brawny arms but that he has an instinctive sense of balance, knows instinctively how to place and distribute the weight of his body. And this is in the nature of things: the human body is strongest in the legs, the arms are merely helpers, auxiliaries. The horizontal-bar specialist, who relies on his arms only, would find it hard to do a hundred 'chin-ups' in succession, especially at high altitude, with a rucksack on his back; and another species of gymnasium expert, the rope-climber, would not climb nine or twelve hundred feet of rope with his arms alone.

In every sport or activity, man has certain abilities and certain limits. In the case of the mountaineer, this means: climb with your legs, use your arms sparingly; because, obviously, you do sometimes come to a pitch – especially on granite – where balance and technique alone are not enough but must be supplemented by great strength in arms and fingers. If arms and fingers have not become tired the matter will go fast and well. But if they have, it will be unpleasant, difficult and in some cases dangerous.

Rock technique

This falls naturally into two parts: free or natural climbing, in which the climber makes use of the rock in its natural state, in all its aspects: slabs, cracks, chimneys; and artificial climbing, in which the lack of holds forces him to have recourse to pitons and the methods associated with them, such as lassoing and 'tyroleans'.

FREE CLIMBING

Depending on the rock formations to be climbed, a distinction can be drawn between exterior climbing, in which the climber ascends on the outer surface of the face, and interior climbing, in which he progresses by means of the fractures in the surface of the slabs. Narrow fractures are called cracks, which enable the climber to raise himself by means of wedging or jamming his feet and hands. Wide fractures are called chimneys, and the climber goes up them by means of *ramonage*, chimney technique.

Exterior climbing

This enables one to climb slabs and arêtes, and to make traverses by following furrows or wrinkles in the rock instinctively, like a child; this spontaneous technique is then developed into a conscious method, using adherence and opposition.

The use of holds. Choose holds for their firmness, convenience and size; then push or pull perpendicularly to the axis of the hold.

Never jump to reach a hold.

Position of the body. The mountaineer climbs as if he was going up a ladder, with his body upright and well balanced over his feet. Both hands should never be stretched upwards at arms' length, simultaneously, but should be at the level of one's face; more exactly, they should be used as when climbing a ladder, with one hand going up while the other stays below, and so on, alternately, while, also alternately, the weight of the body is transferred from one foot to the other.

It not infrequently happens that the beginner, after only a few yards of climbing, finds himself stuck and as if paralysed, splayed out against the rock-face. Beginners always tend to reach up for handholds as high as possible, thinking thereby to make themselves more secure.

Imagine a wall, not vertical but at an angle of 70 degrees; a ladder leaning against it and ending at its top; and a climber on the ladder. If, instead of having one hand at the level of his face and the other only a little higher, he clutches at the rungs at arms' length, shrinks close against the ladder and hangs on desperately, he will reproduce pretty fairly the beginner's uncertain, frustrated plight, which is both physically and psychologically exhausting. A climber who cannot advance, and feels paralysed, becomes anxious; a beginner in this predicament takes a tighter grip on his handholds, puts less weight

As well as physical balance there is another kind, which is even more important: mental balance. This is the keystone of all mountaineering, both in the earliest stages and in the most exacting ascents.

The manner of gripping a hold depends on the equality of the rock. In limestone, where there are many small holds of very uneven contour, the fingers take the form of the hold, with the joints crook'd (1), arched (2) or curled (3). On granite the climber uses mostly cracks (4), or he grips 'leaves' of rock (5), or uses the resistance of one hand (6), or of both hands (7) in the layback.

on his feet (because he is putting more on his hands) and thereby makes the feet less secure. The purchase obtained by the feet, their adherence, varies with the force with which they press on to the rock; the greater the weight applied to them, the better they hold.

To get the beginner back into a safe posture and enable him to go on, it is not enough to tell him to 'unstick' himself from the rock-face; he must be directed to bring his hands down to other, lower holds, and these must be pointed out to him. He will then automatically find himself no longer stuck: his body will be vertical, there will be room for him to raise his legs, he will be capable of visualizing the immediate series of movements to be made, and will be able to carry on climbing.

If, instead of being pressed against the rock-face, the body is vertical, it stands off slightly from the rock. This is essential. For one thing, it enables the climber to see the rock, the holds and the way one hold leads to another. When studying the different ways of attacking a summit you do not go straight to the bottom of the rock-face and take a look from six feet; this would reveal only the first five or six yards of the route. You make your survey from some way off—as Saussure did, for example, before anyone had tried to climb Mont Blanc; his first move was to climb to the Brévent and study Mont Blanc from there. It is the same for every pitch and even every movement: the further the climber's face is from the rock the better he can see the handholds and footholds.

Another thing is that you need room to raise each leg in turn, bending and then straightening the knee so as to bring yourself erect again.

As time goes on and he tackles progressively steeper faces, the experienced climber will keep closer to the rock, so as to avoid continual strain on the arms. He will try always to keep his body vertical, so that his weight is borne as directly as possible by his feet.

What it comes down to, broadly speaking, is that progression always consists of two phases. In the first, the climber's body stands away from the rock so that he can (a) get a better view of the handholds above his head and the footholds at the level of his knees and waist; and (b) have room to initiate his upward movement by raising

8

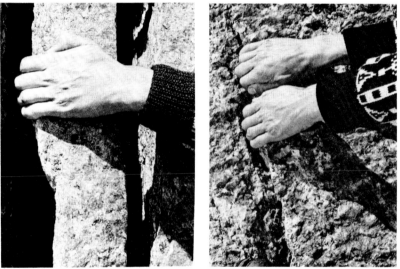

6 7

The pull should always be at right-angles to the hold (8). Finally, use support (9) as a change from traction whenever possible.

his thigh and leg and placing his foot in the next hold. In the second phase, he completes the movement thus initiated and comes closer to the rock, transferring his weight to the uphill foot by moving the uphill knee forwards and straightening the uphill thigh and leg, with the foot as their base. The climber (we repeat) should not *pull* his body up with his arms but raise himself by *pushing* on his feet.

Adherence. This occurs naturally whenever the climber places his foot (or his hand, acting in a support role) in a flat, horizontal hold; adherence is then an effect of weight. If the hold slopes a little towards the downhill side, adherence still results though it may not be equally good. But if the hold is an oblique one a deliberate, forced adherence must be obtained; the foot must press down perpendicularly, or as nearly so as possible, and the greater the pressure the more secure will be the purchase. A nervous, hesitant pressure is completely ineffective; on the contrary, the worse the hold and the smaller the degree of adherence obtained in consequence, the more firmly must one press down, as if one weighed more than one actually does, or as if trying to sink the foot into the surface of the rock.

9

Adherence is easier in proportion to the roughness of the rock and the quality of the grain. Its main function is to permit pushing with the feet, these being kept as flat to the rock as possible, a function which has been enhanced by the invention of Vibram soles. Frictional adherence by the hands is less common; it can occasionally be used, exerted in a vertical direction, on rounded holds, or as a prop on flat or round holds, with the palm of the hand; but its chief uses are during the descent, and in interior climbing (when adherence via the back is also used).

Resistance. This is a sort of forced pressure, obtained by the pull and push of two parts of the body exercised simultaneously in opposite directions. The commonest form of resistance, much used, is obtained by pulling with the hands and pushing with the feet.

Three-point support is of course an important rule: two feet and one hand, or two hands and one foot, so that only one limb is in movement at a time. This is the principle on which safety depends, especially on unsound rock.

There are also subsidiary rules.

The first is to avoid using the knees. A knee, when placed in a hold, swivels or rolls; even worse, it transmits no message to the climber, whereas the foot is a highly sensitive organ and transmits small sensations which matter a great deal. A climber on a pitch he has already climbed before will get quite a different sense of contact if he is using soles of a different thickness from last time, even if they are mounted on exactly the same model of boot. Moreover, giddiness is caused not only by a disturbance in the head but can equally well spring from sensations arising in other parts of the body – particularly the feet – and transmitted to the brain.

It is important to get to know the adhering quality of the soles and to what extent they will hold (1 and 2).

Rigid soles enable the climber to use small footholds (3).

Resistance is a forced adherence obtained by pulling with the hands and pushing with the feet (4).

1

4

The second subsidiary rule is to vary one's movements so as to use different sets of muscles alternately. Hands and arms should change as often as possible from traction to support.

The climber should learn to use holds to either side of his direct line of advance; this enables the feet to provide a firmer base.

Intermediate holds, close to one another, whether for feet or hands, should not be overlooked. They enable the climber to avoid big stretching or straddling movements which upset his balance and entail extra strain on the arms.

Finally, having learnt to climb in a vertical direction the climber should also learn to make traverses. They are extremely useful and the necessity for them often arises, especially on limestone; they allow one to bypass a difficult or impossible place. The mountaineer should be inquisitive; he should look to right and left of him, not just straight ahead. A traverse is an intelligent move in the game, both as a matter of picking the best route and in its detailed execution, which rarely demands strength but is mostly a matter of nicely balanced stepping movements. Traversing often seems like a powerfully vertiginous process, far more so than vertical climbing; it makes one more acutely conscious of the necessity and importance of balance because at every sideways step there is a swing of the body, which is sometimes accompanied by a compensating swing of the leg acting like a tight-rope walker's pole and enabling the trunk to lean towards a hold which is almost out of reach. But the commonest movement is crossing one's legs, as in skating; it gets the body away from the rock-face, makes movement easier, and often eliminates the need for small jumps, which are ugly and unsafe. The hands can

Climbing on limestone is often light, subtle, delicate work, but climbing on granite is much more athletic and must be executed with bold, vigorous technique.

77

be crossed, too, but this should be done only when all other hand positions on a given hold have been exhausted; crossing the hands imparts a twisting tendency.

Another manoeuvre is to change from hand to foot on the same hold when making a rising traverse; this is often followed by a forward swing of the knee, which then takes charge of most of the body-weight; the thigh is then straightened over the shin and foot. There are also various combinations of resistance: between the right and left hands, or between the feet, or between a hand and foot with alternate pushes and pulls; the commonest method being to pull with the hands as they move along a horizontal crack and to push with the feet, which maintain their grip on the slab by pressure.

Fairly often, in traversing as in vertical climbing, one comes to a deep-set foothold, in reverse relief, as it were; either because of an anfractuosity or, in a traverse, under a lip of rock at the bottom edge of a slab. The effect of this is that the bulge of rock just above the hold forces the body outwards.

If the foot is inserted deep into the hold the bulging rock forces the legs to slope backwards, and the knee-joint forces the buttocks further backwards still; the compensating forward bend of the trunk brings the climber tight against the rock, a most inconvenient position in which the strain on the arms makes further movement almost impossible.

But if, on the contrary, only the foremost part of the feet is placed at the edge of the anfractuosity, the ankles can be bent slightly forwards, the knees can be brought into contact with the rock and in some cases will become extra points of support, the buttocks are in their normal position above the feet, the compensating forward bend of the trunk is only slight and the arms do not work nearly so hard to maintain the climber's balance.

Pulling up on the hands. Avoid as far as possible pulling up at arms' length; if this is unavoidable do it quickly, so as to tire the arms for as short a period as possible; and accompany the pull of the arms with a push of the legs.

Whenever you can, extend the pull-up with a push of the hands, simultaneously bringing one foot up to their level and then transferring the weight to it. Remember that in this movement the knee must not only jack-knife upwards but go forwards; merely bringing it upwards produces an imprecise, insecure position, leaving the back of the body out of balance.

Interior climbing

This is a difficult technique, which comes less naturally than exterior climbing. Mountaineers who are ill-acquainted with it waste much effort, trying to advance but being unable to do so. Even more than in exterior climbing, it is essential to plan one's movements carefully, otherwise fatigue quickly sets in. Interior climbing is almost always a combination of pressure and resistance.

Cracks. These are climbed by means of wedging or jamming with the feet and hands. One may also make use of holds on the slabs on each side of the crack, thus combining interior and exterior climbing.

Wedging. A narrowing of the crack is used to take the foot or the fist and, as one puts one's weight on the foot or pulls on the hand, wedging occurs automatically.

Avoid wedging with the knees and elbows; it is decidedly painful, and it is sometimes difficult to get them out again.

The technique of interior climbing is less instinctive and natural than that of exterior climbing. Mountaineers who are ill-acquainted with it expend a great deal of effort to no purpose. It is essential to discern the mechanism of the movements involved and become fully conscious of it, realizing how and why they give a secure purchase. To clarify the technique required for every variety of crack and chimney, it is first demonstrated on perfectly smooth wooden walls and then shown in its practical application on rock, where the climber takes advantage of the slightest holds. Here, a crack is being climbed by a combination of wedging and jamming.

The 'Pas' de la Grande Candelle, on the limestone of the Calanques.

Jamming. This is an induced wedging carried out by the arm, hand, fingers, legs or feet. The principle is to create leverage between the hand and elbow, for instance, for a fairly wide crack, or between the fingertips and the back of the hand for a narrow one, as if one were trying to force the sides of the crack apart.

The layback. This is a combined resistance of the hands and feet. One simultaneously pushes very hard with the feet (usually on a slab) and pulls very hard on the fingers (usually on a 'leaf' of rock), as if trying to pull the 'leaf' away from the rock-face.

Dièdres (dihedrals). These are corners with a flake crack, usually very narrow, which separates a cliff which is peeling off from the main mass of rock. The crack is climbed by wedging or layback, and if there are any holds on the sides of the dièdre they are used too.

Wide-mouthed chimney-crack. The inner side of the body is raised by the wedging and jamming technique, the outer side uses the chimney technique.

Chimneys. These are deep, wide fractures and to negotiate them the climber goes inside, using the appropriate chimney technique, that is, pushing as if he intended to thrust the two walls of rock apart.

There are different chimney techniques, depending on the width of the chimney:

Very narrow chimney: knees-feet resistance.

Narrow chimney: back-knees.

Medium chimney: back-feet.

Very wide chimney: the climber 'bridges' the crack and progresses by right hand and foot resistance on one side and left hand and foot resistance on the other.

Interior climbing demands making the best use of the two walls of the crack or chimney between which the ascent is being effected, and an efficient synchronization of movements. Generally speaking, one should ascend with the back pressed against the smoother of the two walls. Here, as in artificial climbing, even a well-muscled mountaineer will quickly tire if his command of technique is not good.

Interior climbing on the volcanic rocks of the Hoggar range, on the direct route up the west face of the Tezoulaig.

1

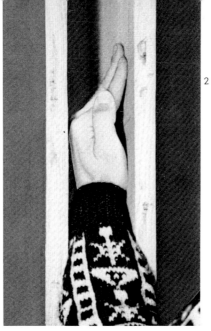

3

2

Jamming is a forced wedging, brought about by resistance between the fingertips and the back of the hand (1–2), or between the hand and elbow (3–4), pushing in opposite directions. The principle is to create leverage.

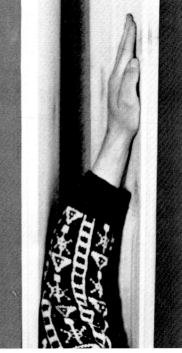

4

Resistance with both hands, as if trying to pull the two walls apart (5–6).

5

6

7

8

Jammed hold with both hands;
each hand naturally tends to twist about
its own axis, and resistance is
simultaneously exerted between the
fingertips and the back of the hand (7–8).

9

10

Resistance between the thumb and the
rest of the hand (9–10).

Wedging with the fist (11).

11

On the Lames de Planpraz, with the Mont Blanc massif in the background.

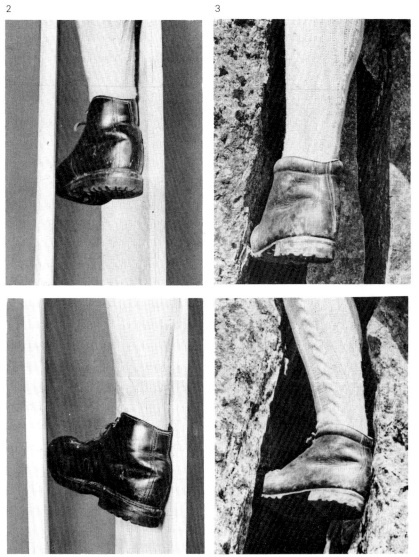

Jamming with foot and knee (1).

Jamming with the outer edge of the front part of the foot and the inner edge of the back of the foot (2–3).

Wedging with the foot in a wide-mouthed crack (4–5).

86

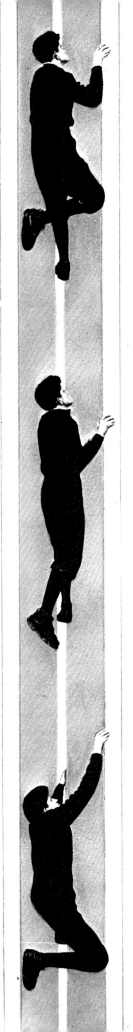

Wide-mouthed chimney-crack: the side of the body which is towards the interior of the crack is raised by jamming and wedging; the outer side uses chimney technique (1–2).

The layback. This is a combined resistance of feet and hands. Security depends on pushing hard with the feet and pulling hard on the fingers (3–4).

Very narrow chimney: feet-knees resistance
(1–2).

Narrow chimney: resistance with
feet-knees, and knees-back (3—4).

Medium chimney: feet-back resistance
('backing up') (5—6).

Next two pages:
Wide chimney: backing up (1—2).

Very wide chimney: transverse chimney
technique (bridging) (3—4).

3   4

In order to gain as much height as possible with the smallest number of pitons, the climber should do his best to put in each piton at arm's length (1) and to stand his full height in the stirrups (2). Having reached the bottom rung of the upper étrier, he recovers the lower étrier (3). Webbing étriers (4) have the advantage of making no noise and not getting wedged in the crack; but an étrier with platforms makes it easier to insert the foot (5).

1

2

3

4

5

On a vertical wall or an overhang it is hard for the climber, after getting beyond the last piton, to stand upright on the top rung of the étrier. To avoid swinging about he should keep one hand very low (the left, in this example) holding the piton (6), while the other ensures lateral stability. Having reached the top rung of the étrier he can cross his feet (as shown below) to maintain his balance while his hands are occupied in driving in another piton, as high up as possible.

Artificial climbing is less beautiful and, appearances notwithstanding, quite often easier than free climbing. But when all the possibilities of free climbing have been exhausted, recourse must be had to pitons and étriers to climb a completely smooth wall with only a narrow crack running up it.

ARTIFICIAL CLIMBING

Since the beginning of mountaineering climbers have used 'the shoulder', but this method is inadequate for a high face or a big overhang. This is why, in addition to lassoing and the 'tyrolean', pitons have been introduced.

'The shoulder'

First of all the second man should belay securely. The operation then takes place in three stages: the leader climbs on to the knees and from there to the shoulders of the supporter, who then helps the leader further by pushing him with the hands or with the ice-axe and by supporting his feet.

Piton technique

This technique, which is often easier than it looks, is, like much else in mountaineering, a question of clear thinking, common sense and balance. It should be used only when all the resources of free climbing have been exhausted.

Inserting pitons. The choice of pitons depends mainly on the character of the rock on which the climb is being made; as a general guide, very hard pitons of alloy steel are suitable for granite, and softer ones for limestone. The hard ones go in without bending and hold fast by wedging; the others, being more malleable, hold by becoming jammed in the rock.

The climber chooses the appropriate pitons as indicated by the depth and width of the crack for which they are intended, and drives them in at the full reach of his arm so as to use as few as possible. The sound they make under the hammer tells him whether they are firmly fixed or not; a clear ringing note indicates a piton well driven in, a dull, hollow sound one which is not holding. Logically, a piton should be put in with its point directed slightly downwards; nevertheless there are pitons which, even when driven in upside down on the horizontal overhangs known as 'ceilings' or 'roofs', get firmly jammed or wedged in the crack and hold firmly enough to function as climbing pitons, though not as support pitons in the event of a fall. Besides, the fact of using a number of pitons means that the strength of the whole is sufficient.

To drive in a piton, a choice has to be made between a light and a

heavy hammer, and one with a short or a long handle. With a fairly heavy hammer (from 600 to 700 gr; from 1 lb 6 oz to 1 lb 10 oz approx.) a piton goes in fairly quickly yet does not buckle, even if made of mild steel, which it would do if a heavier hammer was used; a fairly long handle (25 cm; 10 ins) is preferable to a shorter one but requires more accuracy on the part of the striker.

An important principle in using pitons is that, to provide maximum support, the piton must be positioned and used in such a way that the load placed upon it (including the sudden wrench exerted by a fall) shall act at a right-angle to the shank of the piton. A vertical piton in a vertical crack, even if correctly fixed, may well swivel downwards and pull out under the impact of a load abruptly applied (unless it is jammed firmly in a crack with a sinuous cross-section, or inserted immediately above a narrowing of the crack so that the sudden force cannot make it swivel downwards). This is the reason why horizontal pitons are now almost universal; they work anywhere, especially if the plane of the eye, instead of continuing that of the blade, is slightly rotated, constituting a torsion-arm which helps to absorb the shock of a fall.

A piton should be driven right home, so that the eye comes into contact with the rock. If all the pitons you have with you are too long and will not go all the way into the crack, do not put the snap-link through the eye of the piton; instead either bend the piton downwards (which can be done with a mild steel piton but not with one of the harder type), or else put a self-tightening knot round the piton just where it enters the rock, for which purpose it is better to use webbing rather than line – line has a tendency to slip round the piton (webbing does not, and is considerably stronger). This solution is a lot better than bending the piton, in every case.

To fix a piton, a crack should be chosen with clearly defined square edges. If the only available crack has rounded edges – which would make it easier for the piton to be extracted by a sudden pull, especially if the crack is a shallow one – the same rule applies: do not put the snap-link through the eye of the piton but in a fairly long piece of webbing tied to the piton as close as possible to where the piton goes into the rock. The same should be done if the piton is very short because the crack is very shallow, but in this case the climber will take care to put in the piton with the eye pointing up, not down, so that the webbing is trapped between the rock and the eye of the piton.

In other words, the general rule is that the sudden force, which would come onto the piton if the climber had a fall, must be applied as close as possible to the rock. This is the reason why ring-pitons driven right home sometimes give a better hold than ordinary pitons (those with eyes); the ring is closer to the rock than the centre of the eye would be. This is also the reason why webbing is so effective; a further one is that webbing contributes to absorbing the shock.

Until not long ago we were sometimes reduced, when coping with rather wide cracks, to rigging up combinations of several pitons, or of wooden wedge, piton and the rock itself. But the advent of the American angle-iron pitons, of all sizes, has almost entirely eliminated this necessity.

The American pitons, because of their hardness, neither should nor can be driven in after the same fashion as pitons of softer steel. Yvon Chouinard, the inventor of these extra-hard pitons, advises as follows:

'In the first place, the mistake most often made in the use of these

When the climber is in direct tension on a piton it is difficult for him to rise well clear of this piton by standing on the top rungs of his étrier, even by crossing his feet; it is not only a question of his own balance and fatigue, there is the strain on the piton to think of as well, especially if it is a climbing piton, not a support piton. In the photos on the right, the climber has gone up so far as to bring the junction between rope and harness well above the level of the piton; he must therefore put in another piton, fixing it all the more securely in that it is the one on which the successful conclusion of this pitch depends.

hard pitons is to drive them in too hard. But the way to get the full resistance out of these pitons is not to drive them in right up to the hilt but to position them in such a way that when they come under load they are self-tightening and are incapable of coming out.

'In a vertical crack, the prime desideratum is resistance to downward tilting. The crack must be examined for the place which suits the piton best and supplies a built-in resistance to any change of position. The ideal is a localized broadening of the crack, holding the piton by both edges of the blade. For example, a piton has been badly placed if the blade is pinched on both sides at one point only, a troublesome axis of rotation about which it is free to swivel downwards.

'As a rule, it should be possible to insert only half or three-quarters of the length of the piton into the crack before using the hammer. The next step is to drive it part of the way with the hammer, then to give it a tap from above to check whether it is firm. If necessary, go on driving it in and checking it at intervals by a blow from above, until it is obviously quite firm. At this moment, resist the temptation to hit it just once more: that last, extra blow is the one that makes it hard to get out again afterwards. But if the crack is such that perfect placing simply is not possible, the only answer – especially if the crack is vertical – is to drive it in as strongly as possible with the hammer.

'Always remember that when a piton has been fixed it must be tested before being used. This is done, as we have seen, by one or two light taps from above and from the side. These should not succeed in shifting the piton at all.

'A piton has been fixed perfectly if it stands a load of 2,000 kilos [about 4,400 lb] after being put in by hand and driven home with one blow of the hammer. This is perfectly possible after a little training. But it is advisable to practise putting in these new pitons before using them in actual climbing.

'When knocking a piton sideways to get it out, a mistake frequently made is not to hit it far enough in both directions and to try to loosen it by little taps first on one side, then on the other. The piton must be hit in one direction alone until it has gone as far as it will, then be hit once more in the same direction before being hit from the other side. Care must be taken, however, not to knock it out of shape. To prevent spoiling the shape of the head, hit the forward part of the head as much as possible. In deep cracks, and also when a ring or snap-link is hanging from the eye, the blows should be concentrated on the area where the eye ends and the main body of the piton begins. The fact that the pitons are conical in profile results in their coming out of themselves when they are hit on both sides.'

Another way of extracting a piton is to make a chain out of three or four snap-links, hook a large piton (one of the big angle-iron ones, for example) through the last snap-link, and strike outwards on the head of the large piton.

Support pitons and climbing pitons. The general distinction between these two is that support pitons are those which can be used not only for climbing but also for belaying; they are inserted in the best conditions, in a good sound crack, and must be capable of withstanding a fall, which means they must be at least as strong as the snap-links and climbing rope. Climbing pitons are those which, in the absence of a really good crack, would certainly not hold a fall and are sufficient only to support the climber as he progresses. A climbing piton should be capable of withstanding a little over twice

Artificial climbing can also be used on ice for negotiating vertical or even slightly overhanging surfaces (1).

Chouinard has invented the 'cliffhanger', a hook which can sometimes be substituted for a piton provided there is a flat place just sufficiently large to take it. In some cases it is better not to connect with a snap-link directly through the eye of the hook but to use a loop of line or webbing and put the snap-link through that; this neutralizes any tendency on the part of the hook to swivel about (2).

If the rock is smooth and dense in consistency, the expansion piton is the answer. Here, the belaying rope can be seen in the first snap-link, and the upper end of an étrier in the second (3).

the weight of the climber (the weight of the leader plus the force exerted on the rope by the second man to take the weight of the leader when the latter is in tension on the rope). On climbing pitons, the leader will always use étriers, not direct traction, because in this way his own weight alone will be brought to bear on the piton; moreover, there are certain pitons which, inserted in a horizontal crack, provide an acceptable degree of security as long as traction is in a downward direction, that is to say at right-angles to the axis of the piton; they would come out immediately, however, if the point at which the climber was attached to the rope came opposite the piton, because the piton would then be subjected to a direct outward pull.

Progression on pitons. The piton having been put in, the climber hooks a snap-link onto it and passes his rope through it (or one of his ropes, if he is on a double rope at the time). The rope must go through in the right direction: the end coming up from below should be against the rock (between the rock and the snap-link provided the latter is hanging normally), so that as it goes through the link it points straight towards the leader.

Some climbers prefer to put the snap-link on the rope first and then onto the piton.

In either case, besides taking care that there are no kinks or loops in the rope to prevent it from running freely, make sure that the snap-link itself is suitably located, that is to say hanging free, not wedged slantwise, in the eye of a piton driven in too far or deeply inserted into too narrow a crack; nor should the link be bearing, lever-fashion, on a knob of rock. There must be no risk that the link will open in the event of the climber's falling. In doubtful cases it is best to interpose a length of webbing between the piton and the snap-link. Another way is to couple two or three snap-links together. But webbing is better, provided its strength is at least equal to that of the piton.

Direct traction. By means of the piton he is holding on by, and the rope on which he is pulling, the leader raises himself on the piton he has just driven in; simultaneously the No. 2, by pulling on the rope, helps the leader to come up to the level of the piton and supports him there.

Direct traction can also be used to execute slanting or horizontal traverses on faces which would defy ordinary methods. The rope is put through a snap-link or a length of webbing attached to a piton (or, alternatively, directly through a ring-piton) driven in as high as possible; the leader traverses by pushing with his feet, pulling with his outer hand on whatever holds present themselves, and with the inner hand pushing or pulling on other holds or holding the belaying rope, while the second pays out rope as and when the leader asks for it.

Climbing on étriers. If the rock is without holds (or, equally, if the piton is not very firm) the climber uses an étrier. Each étrier must be equipped with a snap-link which is then attached to the belaying snap-link. Attaching the étrier directly to the belaying snap-link can be troublesome and tiring, particularly when the turn of the second comes; still, this direct connection is feasible except in a few exceptional cases.

The best snap-links for étriers are those without spurs. Certain climbers however prefer the little Cassin snap-links; these, being smaller and slighter, enable one to gain a little extra height, and they are easier to put on. But they are inconvenient to hold, and in artificial climbing without natural handholds this can be a drawback.

If the étriers hung in position by the leader are left there for the second, it is preferable for the leader to put a snap-link onto the

snap-link holding the étrier and another one, for belaying, onto the former. Taking the snap-links off again will be easier for the second climber.

In some cases where the rockface is not quite vertical it is frequently an advantage for the leader, as soon as he has climbed past the piton to which the snap-link holding the étrier is attached, to put his heels, instead of the front of his feet, in the upper stages of the étrier; the lines and rungs of the étrier then hold him against the rock.

Since the rungs of the étriers replace the non-existent footholds in the rock, the climber should raise himself on the rungs exactly as he would on footholds: he should straighten up on his feet, not pull himself up by his arms, which are not meant to perform the movement but to accompany it. The essential movement to be learnt, as Noël Blotti emphasizes in his excellent manual, is to raise oneself from rung to rung of the étrier, including the top one, and even to put one's foot on the piton, *without* pulling with the arms; this is possible whenever the face is a little short of the vertical, say up to about 90 degrees. For one thing, this is excellent practice in sensing one's balance; in addition, it means making the best use of the aids employed in artificial climbing and keeps the number of pitons required to the minimum. Few climbers have mastered this essential movement; they drive in another piton while they are only on the second rung and thus throw away half of the potential which these aids provide.

Immediately an étrier takes the climber's weight – for example when the right foot engages the bottom rung – the étrier comes up close against the rock and it is not always easy to get the left foot onto the second rung; it can even be quite difficult if the first rung happens to be just level with a miniature overhang and the rock above this is vertical, because the upper rungs are then forced flush against the rock. The solution is either for the climber to press his right knee against the rock, so that leverage brings his right foot, and the étrier with it, away from the rock; or he can turn his body sideways on, which likewise has the effect of making it easier to get his foot onto the next rung.

Except in certain cases, overhangs in particular, it is not recommended to put two snap-links onto one piton; it takes too long and is cumbersome.

On the third rung of an étrier with four rungs, or on the middle rung of one with three, the climber can, if need be, rest for a moment by bringing the foot which is on that rung under his body, having first shifted the étrier to a position along the inside of his thigh.

Finally, it is not advisable to sit in an étrier; étriers are for climbing with, not for sitting. If you want to sit, which is the normal thing to do when belaying, there is the *escarpolette* or 'swing' (an étrier with a single, very wide rung of wood, plastic or, which is much to be preferred, of nylon fabric, as in the Robbins model).

Except when the climber is on the underside of a 'roof', the foot which is on the rung of an étrier should be supported against the rock; otherwise he may swing about, which is tiring and awkward. If the face is slightly less than vertical he will be able to put his free foot between the rock and the foot which is in the étrier, and this will enable him to keep his body upright. But whenever an overhang appears the leader will have to resort to direct traction and the technique of the double rope.

The double rope. Two ropes are used instead of one; and these are different in colour, thickness and, it may be, in make. On the other hand, instead of using two ropes each (say) 90 feet in length, a common device is to use a single two-coloured rope 180 feet in length, for example with one half red and the other blue; one advantage being that you can always find the mid-point.

The principle is simple. As the leader progresses, he passes first one rope, then the other – the red and the blue to stick to the example given above – through the snap-links on the pitons he has just driven in, and as he stands upright on one rung after another the second man pulls now the red rope, now the blue one, alternately, and slackens the one he is not pulling, and then uses his belay to hold the leader at the level desired.

The advantages gained by double-roping are considerable.

The leader is continuously supported by direct traction from the second man via the two ropes alternately; this support includes the transition from one piton to the next, which is not the case with

single-roping. When the face is less than vertical this is unimportant, because the leader's weight is supported by the étriers, and his arms have nothing strenuous to do; but it is a different matter on a vertical face or an overhang, for then, even though making the best possible use of his étriers, he has to pull himself up with one hand while pulling the rope up with the other in order to slip it through the snap-link on the next piton, and this can be made very difficult by the friction of the rope against the snap-links and the rock.

The single rope has to go through all the snap-links and turn corners in order to do so, and incurs friction against the rock in its zigzag course from link to link. But with the double rope each rope goes through every other snap-link and follows a much straighter course, with correspondingly less friction.

Finally, the double rope offers the possibility of various related manoeuvres.

Climbing the 'Toit' de Sarre. This overhang is not horizontal like a ceiling but slightly sloping, nearly 100 feet from side to side, with an under-surface of some 80 feet climbing distance. Part of the 'roof' has cracks, the rest requires the use of expansion pitons.

Friction always exerts a troublesome braking-effect, even with the double rope. To reduce it, the leader can use snap-links in twos or even threes instead of singly; or, better still, use webbing instead. Another possibility, which applies to either the single or the double rope, is for the leader to release the rope or ropes from some of the less vital pitons as soon as he has got past them and has reached other pitons, firmly fixed, to which of course he will keep the rope or ropes secured.

However, on certain pitches which are luckily not often encountered, the combined effect of friction and the elasticity of the ropes largely cancels out the tension maintained by the second climber, however much force he exerts.

The leader must then have recourse to certain methods of auto-traction, which can be applied whether he be below or above the piton, or level with it. He can use a line sling, or, which is better, a Prusik knot with or without a snap-link, or a chain, long or short as occasion may demand, comprised of a number of snap-links, fixing one end of this to his harness and the other to the piton. These methods, which are beyond the scope of this book, are described in the highly specialized and very interesting manual by Gianni Mazenga. Noël Blotti's recommendation is to abandon conventional methods in favour of auto-traction étriers; he describes his system in an excellent manual which is of great interest to specialists in artificial climbing.

How the team advances. There are several different ways in which two or more climbers on a rope can make their way upwards.

The leader can climb with two or three étriers which he uses and recovers as he goes. No. 2 does the same. The advantage of this method is that only four or six étriers are required; the disadvantage is that it takes twice as long and is rather tiring.

Alternatively, the leader takes all the étriers with him (as many as fifteen or twenty in some instances) and leaves them in position for No. 2. This is economical in movements and time but needs a large number of étriers, which are heavy to carry.

The best method for both leader and second climber is to use étriers with Griff-Fiffi hooks and grips. The grips are indispensable. This method enables the étriers to be recovered automatically and without fatigue.

Whenever possible, the leader will use webbing slings placed round rock-bollards, which is much less trouble than putting in pitons and simplifies the recovery problem. Or, of course, he can use the metal or plastic wedges which are forced into a crack, a favourite technique with British climbers.

The leader will try to find and set up a belay before the rope is fully extended, so that in the event of his falling during the last few yards of his ascent the second man will have enough rope left to effect a running belay.

For belaying, the leader will firmly drive in two pitons: one high enough to ensure his own security, the other for belaying the second man; in some cases he will add a third piton on which to hang an étrier and Robbins 'swing' (of webbing and fabric), so that he can sit and rest even without a ledge on which to put his feet.

When both ropes are in tension the second starts climbing. Obviously the simplest case is when he finds the étriers already in position and does not have to recover the pitons. In this event, each time he comes to a piton he takes his safety-rope out of the snap-link and raises himself on the étrier until he can stand on the next étrier;

Not infrequently, both men on the rope will be climbing with artificial aids; belaying is then carried out with pitons and étriers.

at this juncture, supported by the leader, he leans down and recovers the lower étrier, and the process is then repeated.

If the étriers are not in position he will have to attach the upper one himself in order to be able to recover the lower. Recovery will be quicker if he has a Griff-Fiffi étrier.

If he has to recover the pitons he will, when necessary, lengthen one étrier by fastening another to it with a snap-link so as to bring himself to the level of the piton to be taken out. Extracting pitons is an ungrateful task, sometimes difficult and in any case tiring; and to reduce fatigue as far as possible the second man must have the best conditions for the job.

He can also put a rope sling with a self-tightening knot on one of the two ropes, which will simultaneously be held fast by the leader; to this sling the second man will attach an étrier by means of a snap-link, and thus make it easier to recover the pitons.

There are certain unusual climbs on which the team can profitably use a third rope. This is a help in a number of ways: for pulling up rucksacks; for providing a handrail (fixed rope); as an auxiliary climbing rope; as an extra rope on which the leader can come directly down to the second, bypassing the pitons; for short abseils; and for pendulums.

Conversely, a single rope may be enough for a climb in which the successive pitches of artificial climbing develop up straight cracks without overhangs, so that the rope is not braked by overhangs or angles of rock.

The fact is that artificial climbing demands a thoughtful, common-sense approach. One has to ask, first, What is the problem? and then, How do we solve it?

Artificial climbing, like chimneys and cracks in free climbing, does not require great exertion providing the climber has a good technique and is able to sense how much strength to apply; failing this, it can be exhausting.

I have several times made the ascent of the east face of the Grand Capucin; most of this is artificial climbing. On one of these occasions I was accompanying a young woman who climbed extremely well but weighed very little. There is no doubt that she could help me very little by pulling on the ropes, and that in belaying me to a piton she could give only token rather than effective support. Yet I believe that I climbed that great rock-face more easily on that day than any other, because I was aware from the start that all my movements had to be carried out with impeccable technique and balance, ensuring maximum safety and economy of effort.

The technique of auto-traction étriers. For climbers who want to tackle big, lengthy overhangs, Noël Blotti has invented (at least, I have not heard of anyone doing it before him) the technique of *étriers d'autotraction.* He explains this in his book *Technique et école d'escalade (Climbing Technique and Training)*; the main points are as follows:

The equipment required is two étriers (three or four rungs each) joined by two small snap-links to two pieces of line of unequal length, and connected to the shoulder-harness. The length of the shorter piece of line is equal to the distance from the harness to the sole of the foot when the leg is at full stretch, in line with the body. The length of the longer piece of line is equal to the distance from the harness to the tips of the fingers when the arm is stretched above the head.

Both pieces of line should be secured with knots directly to the harness, without snap-links.

The procedure is to climb conventionally until reaching a 'roof', and then to belay to the first piton. The étrier is not put onto the snap-link; on the contrary, the longer of the two lines is put through the link, one foot is placed on the lowest rung of the étrier attached to the line, and the weight is progressively transferred onto that foot; the étrier goes down and the climber is simultaneously carried upwards towards the piton (the snap-link acts as a pulley).

The shorter of the two lines is put through the snap-link and the climber goes up as high as he can on the étrier with this line (the lines can run through the same snap-link, or through two).

The advantages are that the climber does not have to pull with his arms but raises himself with his legs alone; and that the second man does not have to belay him.

Moreover, the drawback caused by the friction and stretching of the ropes when threaded through a large number of snap-links, which make it impossible to belay the leader close up under the piton, is eliminated. There is thus a saving in fatigue for both men on the rope.

Belays are of course carried out as usual, without it being essential to use two ropes.

The difficulty of the method lies in the correct placing of the snap-links. This is a question of practice.

The technique comes into its own as soon as the body can no longer stand on the étriers by means of balance alone, without help from the arms; in other words, as soon as the angle of the face exceeds the vertical. And the greater the degree of overhang, the more one notices the saving in muscular exertion.

On granite formations, the overhangs are mostly clear-cut and angular, having originated from large-scale fractures of the rock.

Next two pages: north face of the Grandes Jorasses.

Even at a great height, artificial climbing is neither extremely difficult nor extremely athletic, provided it is carried out with a good technique. The main thing is always to be well balanced and to let most of your weight be carried by the étriers (usually on a bent leg, but that depends on the build and suppleness of the individual climber). At the same time, thanks to the complete shoulder-harness, the climber is fully supported in a sitting or lying position, thus considerably reducing fatigue.

Background: the Grandes Jorasses, the Arêtes de Rochefort, Mont Mallet and the Dent du Géant.

On coming to the end of the overhang, the use of a third étrier, this time of the ordinary kind, enables the climber to regain the vertical position, or to abandon his *étriers d'autotraction* and do the next bit by free climbing.

When ordinary étriers are used, the load on every piton is twice the weight of the climber: namely his actual weight, plus the pull exerted by the second to offset the leader's weight and belay him at the desired level. With *étriers d'autotraction*, the load on the piton is halved, consisting only of the climber's weight.

Here is a variation of the method, based on the fact that the two lines will, in practice, be of about equal length; the distance from waist to sole of foot, and from the waist to the fingertips of the up-stretched arm, being the same in most individuals. This being so, the climber can stand on the first étrier, the line of which goes through the first snap-link, and keep the second étrier for the second snap-link, and so on.

Alternatively, when the climber has straightened up on the top rung of the first étrier, he can, if he wishes, moor himself (by means of a piece of chain or a Fiffi hook) to the snap-link, and thus have both hands free, without strain or effort. It is then easy for him to put a snap-link on the second piton and pass the line through the second étrier.

He then puts his whole weight on to the first étrier, so as to be able to unfasten his 'mooring'; places his foot in the second étrier; transfers his weight from the first étrier to the second, and rises on the second étrier as he did on the first and moors himself again.

The pendulum

When the climber has to make an extensive traverse to negotiate, for example, a slab without the slightest hold, but bordered by two cracks, he performs a pendulum to get from one to the other. To do this, he raises himself as high as possible along the first crack and firmly fixes a piton at full stretch; he then comes down again a few feet and, holding himself on the rope by one hand, pushes off and runs across the slab to grip the second crack with his free hand.

To carry out a pendulum the climber may also use a sling of rope passed either round a firmly wedged chockstone, or round a protruding rock, being careful to see that the sling does not pull off.

Lassoing and rope-throwing

For climbing certain pitches which are absolutely smooth and without cracks, the only method remaining at the climber's disposal is to throw the rope.

Short throw. This may be used on the summit mass of the Aiguille de Roc, for example. Taking a rope of the appropriate length the climber lassos a protuberant piece of rock and then pulls himself up by the arms.

Long throw. The summit mass of the Aiguille de la République, which is 60 feet high, is an example of where this may be used. Instead of lassoing a rock promontory, one throws the rope right over an arête. First throw a strong, light line weighted with a snap-link, or

The pendulum is a movement which is not often used, but which can be enormously helpful on occasion. The pitons must be put in sufficiently high up, so that when the climber makes his swing he will be able to reach the hold for which he is aiming.

preferably with a lead weight; to do this, swing the rope round and round in bigger and bigger circles and then, with a sharp swing at the end of one of these revolutions, hurl the weighted end upwards with a view to its going over the arête and landing on the other side, where another member of the party receives it and pulls on it.

To this line a rappel rope is now attached by a reef knot, which, being flat, will slide easily over the crest. The rappel rope should be shaken as it goes over to prevent it from being much rubbed or braked against the rock. Then, by the same method, the party rope is attached to the rappel rope. The second climber secures this from the other side of the arête by fixing it to a large bollard or a firm piton.

The leader can then pull himself up this rope by his arms, using the most favourable, that is to say the less steep, side. He may also use the Prusik loop method which is safe but slow; long-drawn-out, therefore tiring. It is better, if one can do it, to hoist oneself up the rope with speed and decision so as to remain with all the weight on the arms for the shortest possible time.

'Tyroleans'

These may be used on (for example) the Clochetons de Planpraz, or the Guglia de Amicis in the Dolomites. The rope is thrown either directly or by means of a weighted line. Once the rope is hitched onto the point to be reached, or on one of its protuberances, it must be pulled taut and fixed firmly to the stance. There are two ways of making the actual passage:

Seated tyrolean. For short passages. The climber straddles the two ropes and crosses seated between them, leaning slightly forward.

Hanging tyrolean. For long passages. One knee is passed over the ropes and the climber progresses by pulling himself along with the hands.

In both cases it is wise to belay to the tyrolean ropes by means of a snap-link.

Left: Tyrolean, seated position, on the Clochetons de Planpraz. Right: Tyrolean, suspended position, on the Guglia de Amicis, in the Dolomites. In the background, some way below the climber and slightly to the right, are the Cime di Lavaredo.

On eas
suppo
the tru
down

If the
descer
On this
that it

sling which goes round the protruding rock or through the piton; put one end of the abseiling rope through the sling and pull it through bit by bit (taking care to pull the inner rope, the part which is between the sling and the rock); then make the throw. This is a slow, protracted, superfluous, tiring operation.

In my opinion the following method is better: make the sling and tie it; if it is a big one, put one half of the rope, still coiled in a skein, through the sling in one go; then throw. If the sling is a small one, do not make the knot straight away; first throw the rope, keeping hold of the middle of it (if there is any danger of the rope's escaping, put the middle of it round the bollard or through a snap-link on the piton on which the sling, still unknotted, is hanging); put the middle through the sling and then complete the latter by making the knot. This avoids putting the whole of one half of the rope through the sling.

An even quicker method is this: one climber makes it his job to throw the rope while the other prepares the sling; this deals with the first abseil. In subsequent ones the sequence is: on completing the first abseil the leader fixes a sling round a rock bollard or on a piton; when the second climber has come down, one end of the rope is passed through this sling and is pulled down.

Each end of the rope can be thrown separately if the rope is two-coloured, or if two ropes of equal length, joined together, are being used; or both ends can be thrown at once if the middle is not marked, or if two ropes of different lengths, joined together, are being used.

If two ropes joined together are being used—whether equal or unequal in length—the part which includes the knot should be undermost in relation to the sling, hanging down against the rock.

The rope should be coiled neatly and evenly and then thrown outwards so that it uncoils without getting tangled. Make sure that the rope does not get caught up and that the two strands reach the lower stance properly.

Methods of roping down. Increasingly, and quite rightly, climbers are roping down on a snap-link or a descendeur. But it is essential to know the traditional procedure as well—because an occasion may arise when you have neither of these; or because you may have to abseil on two ropes of unequal length, so that the knot makes the use of a snap-link or a descendeur impossible.

Traditional method ('S' abseil). From the sling, the rope (which is double, of course) passes under one thigh, comes up obliquely across the chest and goes over the opposite shoulder—for example, under the right thigh and over the left shoulder. In this case the left hand holds that part of the rope which is in front of the body and the right hand holds the part which comes round the back of the body after passing over the left shoulder. The forward (i.e. left) hand must never be tightened round the rope, nor must it support even a fraction of the body's weight. The weight is entirely supported by the braking action of the rope round the body, and this action is regulated by the rear (i.e. right) hand.

At first, the climber must teach himself to keep the forward hand open and to observe the fact that it is the rear hand which controls the operation; indeed, contrary to the beginner's instinctive reflex, it is quite possible to leave go altogether with the forward hand, the only function of which is to maintain the balance of the upper part of the body; but the rear hand must never let go. If the climber wishes to brake more sharply he must bring the rear hand forward, so that the rope comes under the right armpit; friction of the rope between the right upper arm and the upper part of the rib-cage increases the braking action, which can be increased yet further by pressing the arm against the body (and further still if, again by means of the right hand, the rope is passed between the thighs).

The climber must train himself to be equally capable of abseiling with his right thigh and left shoulder, or left thigh and right shoulder. And he must take care to protect his neck by turning up or pulling up his shirt, pullover and anorak on the side where the rope comes against it; if necessary he should use a scarf, handkerchief or glove as extra padding. This not only avoids burns but prevents the rope from compressing a major nervous plexus which lies close to the surface just here and is poorly protected by nature. Such compression can either bruise the nerves or may even put them out of action (neurapraxia) and thus paralyse the upper limb on the side of the body concerned (Dr Gailland, in *Les Alpes,* June 1967). A mishap of this type has perhaps been responsible for cases in which a mountaineer has unaccountably let go of the rope when abseiling. It follows that the 'S' abseil should never be used without the climbing rope being belayed – beginners, at any rate, should always take this precaution; and the depression above the collarbone should always be well protected.

Roping down on a snap-link. This is more comfortable than the 'S' abseil, especially if the ropes are wet. Place both legs in a sling of rope, then join in front, between the legs, the two sides of the sling with a snap-link (preferably one with screw closure) or, better, with two snap-links (so arranged that their opening sides face in opposite directions); the abseil rope goes through the links and then over one shoulder as in the 'S' abseil. (If two snap-links are used the abseil rope does not have to make such a sharp bend and is less subject to wear.)

If the climber is using a complete shoulder-harness the sling is unnecessary.

Roping down on a descendeur. The descendeur was originally invented by Pierre Allain; many other people have since brought out their own models.

When a descendeur is used there is no friction between the rope and the body – a delightful improvement, which greatly reduces fatigue; complete braking can be applied at any moment, the descent is smooth and after a little practice only one hand need be used.

The descendeur does, however, possess two slight drawbacks: though not heavy (only 150 gr, or $3\frac{1}{2}$ oz) it is an extra item to carry; and it inflicts more wear on the ropes than does ordinary abseiling. On the other hand, it is extremely helpful in rescue-work.

Variations. Between abseiling with a snap-link and with a descendeur there are intermediate methods which can be broadly labelled as adaptations of the snap-link method. The simplest consists of two snap-links arranged crosswise, one vertically and the other transversly. Then there is the Salewa snap-link, on one side of which there is an arm pivoting in a plane at right-angles to the longitudinal snap-link. Finally, in the Magnone descendeur the transversal link is replaced by a rounded, specially-shaped metal plate.

Starting the descent. This is the trickiest part. Grasp both parts of the rope, as low down as possible and vertically beneath the point of attachment (so that the sling has no chance of slipping off the protruding rock); holding them with one hand, use the other to arrange the ropes carefully in the manner already described; then put weight

When roping down, it is a good thing for the learner to stop for a moment (as he will already have done in free climbing), in order to observe just how and why he is securely supported by means of the lower hand, which controls his sliding down the rope.

The simplest method of abseiling is the 'S' abseil (1); the most convenient is that employing a sling and snap-link (5) or a descendeur. Always turn slightly to one side and come down without jerking on the rope; the feet should make a smooth succession of steps down the rock-face (2–6).

1

5

2

4

6

Braking is effected by the rear hand. The forward hand should not grip; it should function only to maintain the balance back-to-front of the upper part of the body (3–7). If a stronger braking action is required, use the 8 abseil, in which the rope coming from the shoulder is brought round the thigh.

3

7

on the ropes and sit in them, otherwise they tend to stray out of position. From the outset, note that the lower hand is the one which commands and controls the abseiling process. At first, that hand should slightly raise the rope, which is hanging down; subsequently, on the contrary, it will control its movement. If the climber is making a belayed abseil, that is to say if he is still roped up on the climbing rope, he must put the latter on one side at the outset so as to ensure that the two ropes do not become entangled. If the start of the abseil is a difficult, delicate one, from some distance below the point of attachment, begin from a sitting position, facing sideways, then turn facing the rock.

The descent:

1. Come down *steadily*–no jerks or lurches–exactly as if you were walking, not as if running or jumping. An abseil is not a succession of little skips but of steady steps down the rock-face, without seeking footholds.

2. Come down *slowly,* without stopping. A fast descent is not only dangerous to the climber himself but bad for the ropes: they heat up, wear excessively and are quickly weakened.

3. Come down with the body slightly away from the rock; do not, however, bend your legs at a right-angle to the trunk, as is sometimes recommended. In that position the climber is not balanced, and balance is essential in roping down, as in everything else in climbing; his weight must be vertically below the point of attachment, in other words he must be sitting on the rope (whether on the rope itself or the sling). The knee-joints should be bent but not stiff and the legs should be vertical; only the front of the feet should bear against the rock and gently push the climber away from it.

4. After a little practice, it is preferable to rope down not facing the rock but turned slightly to one side, so that you can see where you are going.

Recovering the rope. The first climber to come down sees whether the rope is running well, so that, if it is not, the second can make the necessary adjustments. The last man should separate the two strands as he comes down; the easiest way of doing this is for him to put a snap-link onto his harness or sling, and to pass one of the two strands of the abseil rope through it. If two ropes of unequal length, knotted together, are being used for the abseil, making it impossible to rope down on a snap-link or a descendeur, the snap-link used for separating the two strands must take the strand which does not include the knot.

Once he is down he throws the strands apart and pulls on the one which is against the rock where it leaves the sling. Just when the rope is about to come out of the sling he can give it a slight jerk so as to flick it forward; this helps it to fall clear and not get hitched up.

Self-belaying while roping down. This applies to the first climber in the event of his having to rope down without being belayed, and to the last. One possibility is to put a snap-link on the harness or waist-sling and pass the abseil rope through this link. But the best way is to use a sling which is shorter than his outstretched arm, put it round the abseil ropes with a self-tightening knot and fasten it to a snap-link on his harness or waist-sling. (Care must be taken that the self-tightening knot is always within reach of his hand; if it is too high up it is out of his control and may halt his descent.)

The climber keeps the self-tightening knot running free with his forward hand during the descent, and can belay himself by halting his movement and bringing weight to bear on the Prusik.

Technique on snow and ice

On rock, the ability to get a good hold with the hands and then place the foot on it gives a feeling of safety and confidence. Snow and ice, on the contrary, are alien, slippery elements, with nothing to hold on to. Hence, even more than on rock, it is essential while learning the technique to acquire a good sense of balance. Whatever the angle of the slope the body must remain vertical, with the centre of gravity passing through the feet.

It is obvious that the beginner should from the outset make use of his ice-axe, which constitutes his third point of support; but, after each new movement has been studied, I advise him, as I have already said, to go through the same movements without the ice-axe to help him. In this way he will automatically have his body in a vertical position, his crampons will bite well, and he will become aware of his balance and find himself secure – often to his own surprise; he will also find out why he is secure and to what degree he is so. Conversely, he will realize that if his centre of gravity were to pass outside his base, that is to say, his feet, he would lose his balance and fall. On rock this is only relatively important, because there are handholds available by which he can support himself; but on ice, except in rare cases, there are none. That is why, even more than on rock, it is not enough just to learn the actions; it is necessary to bring each new experience to the level of consciousness. In this way stability will be quickly acquired and the synchronization of movements will come naturally.

Like the ice-axe, crampons are a source of security, but it will be very profitable for the beginner to train himself to take off his crampons and strike out just with his feet on snow slopes up to an angle of 40 degrees, and cut steps on ice slopes of 50 degrees; incidentally, when wearing crampons one cannot tell whether a step is well cut, that is to say whether the foot feels firmly and securely placed in it. It is true that crampons were invented in response to a need, but the experiment I recommend will be excellent training for the future mountaineer in two ways: he will become conscious of his own degree of balance and stability, and he will gain in ease and confidence when he finds himself able to do without crampons when crossing a gully of snow or ice which may on occasion be encountered in the middle of a rock climb. Once the beginner has understood this he will progress rapidly, and instead of feeling an aversion to ice will be as much at ease on it as on rock. I would even go so far as to say that balance acquired on ice will be useful to him on granite and even more so on limestone, where everything depends on finesse and balance.

Due to the activities of climbing-schools, young climbers are more often rock climbers than ice mountaineers, but if they would learn ice work as they learn rock climbing they would understand that it is less difficult to become a good ice mountaineer than a good rock climber.

Arrival at the Col de la Brenva, in the Mont Blanc massif.

When, in 1955, we were making the film *Starlight and Storm*, conditions on the north faces were extremely bad. The lower snow slope of the Grandes Jorasses, usually pleasantly snow-covered, was a mass of smooth, slippery ice, strewn over with powdery snow which did not hold. There were four of us: Maurice Baquet, Georges Tairraz, Paul Habrah, with whom I had made the ascent three years previously, and myself. Paul was behind, double-roped at 100 feet. I therefore ran out the rope for 100 feet, then, having absolutely no belaying point to enable Paul to join me, I asked him to unrope and rope only singly so that I could go up another 100 feet and thus reach, above me, a bit of rock which was sticking out of the ice, from which I should be able to belay him. But when I reached this bit of rock I saw that it was round and quite useless. Paul then added the Baquet-Tairraz connecting rope to our rope and I went up another 60 feet; then, in the face of the worst possible conditions, the impossibility of belaying here and the lateness of the hour, I decided to turn back. With this the great difficulties began: I had to come down this steep ice-slope, which was as smooth as a ski-jump, without the least anchorage, while my companions were themselves on the slope, on small steps.

Later my companions told me of their intense disquiet while, 260 feet above them, I broached this delicate descent down that plunging incline. If I had slipped, not only would they not have been able to hold me, but I would have tugged them violently and carried them down with me.

I began to make the necessary movements with great caution but suddenly realized that the first necessity was that I should remain stably balanced when I was letting one leg down and gently transferring the weight of my body from one foot to the other. The ice was extremely slippery, the powdery snow was flying about and running down the slope, I had no hold whatsoever for my hands; I was acutely aware that my centre of gravity must not be allowed to pass outside my feet, even by an inch...

SNOW AND ICE

The main snowfalls occur in winter and spring. If the temperature is above freezing point the snow comes down wet, heavy and dense, in large flakes of agglomerated crystals, but at high altitudes, where the temperature is often below freezing point, the snow falls powdery, dry and light. The new covering contains a large proportion of air and settles fairly quickly, but the sun, the cold wind or the *Föhn* soon comes to play with it, filling up crevasses or making snow-bridges, causing avalanches or building cornices, crusts, shelves, waves, ripples ... Thus, little by little, under this action, combined with frost by night and thaw by day, the snow is gradually transformed and settles firmly to give a regular, coherent surface which is good for climbing. However, it will go on changing every day, according to the weather, temperature and orientation, and the climber will encounter four different consistencies, ranging from very soft to very hard.

Soft snow. This may be fresh powdery snow, fresh wet snow, partially melted snow, sticky snow or slush.

Hard snow. This is excellent for ascent. The climber kicks out with the tip of his boot if he is rising directly, or with the uphill sides of

On the north face of the Matterhorn.

Next two pages:
Cornice on the Arête Midi-Plan.

Ice-axe in the walking-stick position on the ascent.

Ice-axe in the walking-stick position coming down.

Ice-axe in the glissade position.

the soles if he is climbing obliquely. The different kinds of hard snow are: crusted snow, spring snow, 'soufflée' snow and névé snow softened on the surface by the sun.

Frozen snow and granular ice or sérac ice. The foot does not bite into this or bites only very poorly. This also applies to impacted snow, névé which has not been softened, certain kinds of 'soufflée' snow, sérac or glacier ice which has not been covered by fresh falls of snow. Ice is particularly slippery after rain.

Gully ice. This is extremely hard, with a glassy appearance, formed by the consecutive action of thawing and refreezing; very difficult to negotiate.

Technique, then, will be determined by the quality of the snow or ice, but the steepness of the incline will also have to be considered. Slight slopes are those of up to 25 degrees. These figures, however, are only an indication, for it is easier to scale an ice wall of 55 degrees under favourable conditions than a slope of 45 degrees on unstable snow.

The ice-axe is the tool which makes progress on snow and ice possible. As for crampons, although they are not always indispensable – and the mountaineers of the 'Heroic Age' made some remarkable ice ascents without crampons – they do facilitate ascents enormously and, at the same time, give a high degree of security. However, the climber should never misuse them, and in certain cases he is better without them, for the feet are lighter; when making an ascent on snow, the extra effort needed to disengage the points is eliminated and when coming down the danger of the snow balling-up on the feet is avoided. Finally, moving without crampons gives a feeling of balance and freedom.

THE ICE-AXE

The ice-axe is used for cutting steps; as a means of belaying; for sounding purposes, to detect crevasses hidden under snow-bridges; for glacier climbing; and for glissading down.

How to hold the ice-axe:

This varies according to the angle of the slope and the quality of the snow.

The 'walking-stick' position. The ice-axe is held in one hand, like a walking-stick. The hand goes round the head of the ice-axe with the palm on the adze; the point is directed forwards and slightly outwards. On a traverse, the ice-axe is on the uphill side.

The glissade position. The name comes from the position in which the ice-axe is held on a glissading descent, but the position is frequently used for ascending traverses on medium slopes of hard snow or ice, and sometimes when descending slightly steeper slopes.

The ice-axe is held in both hands, approximately horizontally in front of the climber, with the point piercing the snow and the pick directed forwards.

The hand which is further from the slope (downhill hand) holds the head of the ice-axe, with the palm resting on the adze. This hand exerts an uphill pull. The hand nearer the slope (uphill hand) grasps the handle of the ice-axe near the ferrule of the point, and gives support.

Depending on the degree of steepness, the length of the handle and the mountaineer's height, the uphill hand is slid towards or away from the point; on a gentle slope the hand is further from the point, and nearer to it on a steep slope.

The glissade position is used mainly on traverses on medium and steep slopes.

It is also used for coming down facing the slope, whether straight down or more or less obliquely. In these cases the anchor-point should be as low as possible, to the climber's right or left. The ice-axe is not in front of the climber but to one side, either to left or right, in a direct descent, but on the uphill side in an oblique one.

The adze-head position. The ice-axe is held by the adze, in one hand, and the pick is thrust anchor-fashion as deep as possible into the snow. The handle points straight downhill.

The adze-head position is used for climbing steep or very steep slopes; if the line of ascent is direct or only slightly oblique, the climber faces the slope.

The anchor position. The ice-axe is strongly anchored by the point, in front of the climber, at about the level of his head; the point is downhill.

To obtain the anchoring effect the thumb and index finger of the uphill hand curl round the adze from underneath, and the other fingers of that hand grasp the head of the ice-axe. The other hand grasps the handle just above the ferrule.

This point can be driven in even more securely by holding the handle with one or both hands just above the ferrule. The point having been thus anchored, the uphill hand goes round the head of the ice-axe in the manner just described.

The anchor position is used on steep and very steep slopes, for ascending, descending and traversing.

People are sometimes surprised to see what a secure hold the anchor position gives when well executed. But this effectiveness depends absolutely on keeping the pick really sharp, and on the serrations on the point going right down to the tip.

The brake position. This position, which is used for glissading, is very like the anchor position, except that the body is held more compactly and takes firm support from the point of the ice-axe by means of the uphill hand.

The shaft position. The ice-axe, held in one or both hands, is thrust in directly in front of the climber, like a stake, with the side (the flattish part) of the handle facing him.

The handle is driven in more or less deeply, depending on the consistency of the snow. But it should always go as deep as possible. The pull should be exerted close to the snow.

The shaft position is used for steep and very steep slopes and for bergschrunds, on hard snow and especially on deep snow.

The handrail position. On the descent, with the climber facing outwards, the ice-axe is held out to the side, in one hand, with the point uphill and the pick downhill. The hand grips the handle near the ferrule. The anchor-effect is supplied by the pick, while the handle remains clear of the snow and parallel to the line of descent. As the climber comes down, his hand slides along the handle as far as the tongues of the socket; the ice-axe is then withdrawn. The pick is the only point of support.

The handrail position is used on medium and steep descents, on hard snow and on ice.

The support position. The ice-axe has two points of support: the

Ice-axe in the adze-head position.

Ice-axe in the anchor position.

Ice-axe in the support position.

point and the pick, the latter being on the uphill side. The handle is held in one hand, at or near the point of balance. The point (spike) of the ice-axe bears down on the snow.

The support position is used on the descent, either in line with the slope or in a succession of more or less oblique lines. On steep slopes the handle is parallel to the line of descent. On an oblique descent, the ice-axe is on the uphill side, with the point higher than the pick.

STEP-CUTTING

The ice-axe

An ice-axe which anchors efficiently is sometimes hard to cut steps with; and conversely, an ice-axe which is good for cutting steps does not always provide first-rate anchorage.

In fact, the ice-axe is at once a combination of the axe, as used for chopping wood, and the *sapi,* the pointed tool which the woodcutter of Savoy uses for fixing wooden shingles.

Many years ago, when crampons had not been invented and mountaineers had to do much more step-cutting, they had something which was literally an 'ice-axe', in which what is now the adze was shaped like an axe-head.

An ice-axe which anchors well has a slender pick (to enable it to penetrate easily) with serrations all the way down to the tip (to make it hold well); sometimes an ice-axe of this type (the Charlet Super-Conta, for instance) almost surprises one by going in so easily and holding so firmly, even on very hard ice.

In order to cut well, an ice-axe should not make a small, deep hole and stick there, but should chop and fashion the ice and clear away the pieces so as to cut out a step quickly and well. With this in view, Grivel has recently brought out an ice-axe in which the pick does not come to a point but stops short, ending in a blade 2 cm (0·8 in) high; guides who have used it say it cuts magnificently.

Just as crampons vary (points long or short), and pitons (mild or hard steel), and rucksacks (with or without pockets on the outside), and snap-links (with different types of catch) – indeed, as everything, not only mountaineering equipment, varies if it has to serve more than one purpose, so, inevitably, ice-axes vary too.

Holding the ice-axe. Cutting with both hands gives greater strength and accuracy. The hands hold the handle near the ferrule; the climber should train himself to cut with either hand leading. In the main, the rear hand contributes strength; the front hand, precision. How far the axe is raised will depend on the quality of the ice; the movement originates in the shoulder joint, is transmitted by the upper arm and developed and directed by the forearms and wrists.

Cutting can also be performed one-handed, and here again one should train oneself to cut equally well with either hand. The hand should be a little way further up the handle from the ferrule; the forearm describes a wider arc but the upper arm also comes into play.

Where to make the steps. Unlike climbing on rock, where the mountaineer can make use only of the holds already there, on ice he is free to carve his way where and as he pleases; it is up to him to

Some ice climbs seem dull when the slope is uniform, but very often the going is varied and offers situations more marvellous than those encountered on rock.

128

profit from this liberty. To this end he should study the terrain carefully; for example, the slope will not necessarily be uniform; here and there it may be slightly convex or concave or undulating – in short, steeper or less steep. Again, a yard to this side or that, the ice may be harder or softer; or there may be stratifications of the ice of which advantage can be taken. In other words, do not begin cutting steps from one point to another until you have had a good look, taking stock of the orientation of the slope and gauging the conditions so as to pick the best route. This kinship with nature, these thoughtful deductions, produce a powerful and intimate pleasure.

Whether about to cut horizontal steps for an oblique route, or 'stoup' steps for a direct ascent, visualize the sequence of movements, foresee where each foot is going to go and make sure that every step is so placed that it is easy to come up on it. The distance between steps should be such that the weakest climber on the rope can move from each to the next without too much effort or any risk of losing his balance.

If the same route is going to be used on the way down, make the steps closer together; after cutting three or four, try coming down them and add extra ones if necessary.

Cutting steps in ice

Traditional method: horizontal steps, oblique progression.

Position of the body. The precondition of good step-cutting is that the climber feels well balanced. If the slope is too steep he should begin by cutting a hold for the uphill hand, then carry on cutting with the downhill hand.

The body, bent slightly forward, should remain in the vertical axis, that is to say it should not lie against the slope; this is particularly true with regard to progression but equally so with regard to cutting, even if only to ensure that the ice-axe comes down vertically, as it should – or, indeed, canted slightly outwards. On the other hand, it is pleasant now and again to lean the uphill shin and knee against the slope as an aid to balance.

Cutting. The task consists of cutting steps for the right and left feet alternately. Procedure:

1. Sketch the base of the step with short horizontal blows of the ice-axe from front to rear.

Cutting horizontal steps.

1. Decide where to cut the step and aim the ice-axe carefully;
2. Cut the ice away with vertical strokes;
3. Hollow out the step with oblique strokes of the pick;
4. Enlarge and smooth the floor of the step.

Moving in steps on the ascent. As you change your direction, cut a step, no larger, but deeper, to accommodate the toes of both feet.

2. Attack the ice with vertical strokes of the adze, working from front to rear; never hit twice in the same place, as this would tend to make the ice-axe stick in. Then change from adze to pick, striking obliquely; hollow out the step, widening its base and making its floor slope slightly downwards from front to back.

3. Smooth the floor of the step, and clear away the loose chips with the adze.

A well-cut step should be a shade longer than the climber's foot and should be made with the minimum number of strokes.

Cutting in soft ice or very hard frozen snow. The first stage, i.e. sketching the outline of the step, can be omitted.

An alternative method. Attack the ice directly with horizontal and oblique strokes alternately, working inwards from front to rear. This is slightly quicker but requires greater skill and accuracy.

Cutting 'stoup' steps. These are used when the line of advance is straight up the slope; their main application is for negotiating short,

steep walls of snow or ice. The more abrupt the wall, the more necessary it is to cut steps beforehand, from the bottom, before getting onto the wall itself; up to three, on a very steep one.

The steps should not be in a straight line but slightly staggered, to left and right alternately, so that the feet follow them easily.

Attack the ice at right-angles to its surface, working from top to bottom of the step, using the pick of the ice-axe to make a hollow resembling a stoup (i.e. the small, rounded niche, a basin for holy water, in the wall of a church). The hollow should widen towards the bottom, to accommodate the front of the boot. (For coming down a very steep wall, enlarge and modify the hollow to make room for the calf and ankle.)

An awkward feature of 'stoup' steps is that the bits and pieces fall

Descent in steps. The tricky part is moving the inside foot downwards; while doing this, the outside leg must be well bent.

133

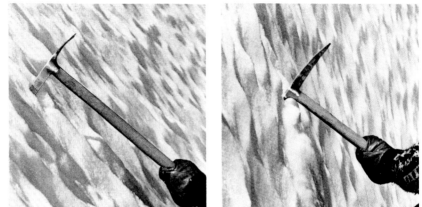

Cutting 'stoup' steps.

on to the climber while he is cutting. Still, the technique is one which enables rapid progress to be made, especially on hard snow.

Gully ice. This is glassy and very hard; the trickiest kind to cut, because it chips easily. Even more than in the case of granular ice it is important not to give two blows with the ice-axe in the same spot – or even one over-vigorous blow; there is a difference in the amount of vigour with which the ice-axe is wielded, though the technique, for either horizontal or 'stoup' steps, is the same as before. You begin by carefully outlining the step, and particularly its base, with little taps; only after this can you cut more energetically. The strength of the step can very often be gauged from the sound; if the blow gives a hollow ring, the ice is on the point of breaking up.

Cutting steps in hard snow. Cutting is unnecessary; a single sharp kick is enough to break the crust and make an adequate

Moving in 'stoup' steps.

Cutting a handhold.

notch. This type of snow – a species of breakable crust known as *'neige "à bout de pieds"'* – can be climbed either direct or by traversing. But if severe frost during the night has made the crust too hard, or if it is névé or springtime snow which the sun has not had time to soften slightly, steps will have to be cut. This is easier than on ice. There are two ways of doing it. Either use both hands, vigorously scraping the surface of the snow with the adze-head of the ice-axe until an adequate platform for the foot emerges; or, with one hand (the uphill hand), swing the ice-axe like a pendulum, using the adze-head to attack the snow at a very flat angle and lifting the elbow well at the end of the movement so that the adze-head does not remain lodged in the snow. The flatness of the stroke forms the 'tread' of the step.

Moving in the steps. In passing from one step to the next, the

Next two pages:
Among the séracs and crevasses of the
Allée Blanche.

135

1

2

position of the ice-axe (walking-stick, glissading position, adze, anchor, etc.) is determined by the steepness of the slope.

As for the action of the legs, after placing a foot (which now becomes the uphill foot) in the newly cut step the whole weight of the body should be transferred to it. The transfer is effected by inclining the upper part of the body forwards so that its weight comes onto the uphill knee, which must likewise be bent well forward and which acts as a pivot; then raise yourself by straightening the knee. The principle is exactly the same as on rock–transfer the weight from one foot to the other by bending the knee forward and using it as a pivot; and, whenever possible, push yourself forward, using the ice-axe in the support position rather than pulling oneself up on the anchor or shaft position.

When you are moving on horizontal steps and the moment comes to change direction, cut a step, not larger, but deeper, to accommodate both feet, facing the slope.

Cutting half the number of steps. With crampons: cut steps for the uphill foot only; the downhill foot holds by means of its crampon. Advance with the ice-axe in the glissading or anchor position.

Without crampons: a really good step is cut for the uphill foot; a notch is sufficient for the downhill foot. Advance with ice-axe in the glissading position or anchor position.

Cutting handholds. This is necessary on very steep slopes. Do not wait to get into a critical or uncomfortable position before starting to cut handholds. At the beginning of the difficult passage, while still standing on a very good step, cut two or three handholds in advance, at suitable distances.

In cutting the first handhold, both hands can be used. The mountaineer can then place one hand in it to keep his balance, and cut the rest of the handholds with his other hand.

The method of cutting the hold is to start it with little horizontal blows with the pick of the ice-axe, so as to make a hole. Then cut with adze and pick alternately, raising the handle so as to hollow out a downward-pointing hole; continue till it is deep enough.

Cutting steps during the descent. This is difficult and tiring; fortunately it is not often necessary. The climber should lean well forward, so that if humanly possible he can use both hands; this makes for accurate, effective work.

To move down from one step to the next, use the ice-axe in the glissading position or support position.

If you are following the steps which were cut for the ascent, and they are too far apart, use them for the uphill foot only; for the downhill foot you can either rely on the crampon or cut small supplementary steps.

THE USE OF CRAMPONS

Crampons frequently come into use. Practically speaking, they are used on all slopes of ice or frozen snow exceeding 30 degrees, and are even sometimes a great help on rock covered with verglas.

Putting on the crampons. This often has to be done in the dark, so it is wise to practise it in advance. It is important to remember that the crampons must fit the boots perfectly, so attention is necessary if either the crampons or the boots have been changed.

It is inadvisable to try and place the crampon underneath the boot; on the contrary, the foot should be placed on the crampon, which has first been laid flat on the snow or ice, with all the fastenings laid outwards. The next thing is to tighten the straps to the right extent: if they are too tight they may restrict the circulation and cause frostbite; if too loose, the crampons are not fixed firmly and may either turn sideways or even come off.

Moving in crampons. At first, take care to keep the feet and legs slightly apart so that the crampons do not catch in the stockings or the gaiters. Never run; firmly control all your movements and, above all, your balance.

In the use of crampons the ice-axe has an important part to play. Its position will depend on the steepness of the slope.

The technique of using crampons. There are two very different techniques, theoretically opposite but in practice complementary, both because of variations in the terrain and because they cut down fatigue by using different muscles in feet and legs.

The first technique is the 'all-points' or 'flat-footed' method. Crampons with ten vertical points are used and the technique consists of making all the points bite as deeply as possible, to which end the boot-soles are presented perfectly flat to the slope, however steep it may be, by means of acute flexion of the ankles, the body remaining vertical; in steep places the climber no longer faces the slope but turns sideways to it.

The second technique is the 'leading-points' method. These crampons have twelve points. Invented in 1931 by Laurent Grivel, guide and blacksmith at Courmayeur, they retained the traditional articulation halfway along the frame and had ten vertical points and, at the toe, two almost horizontal points.

In the last few years, the Austrian and German glacier climbers have been using rigid, unarticulated crampons made in one piece, with eight vertical points at the rear, two slightly angled points at the front (replacing a pair of vertical points), and two almost horizontal points at the very front.

The 'leading-points' technique consists of going straight, not obliquely, up even the steepest slope; as the slope gets steeper the climber relies exclusively on the leading points. It is a more natural, indeed an instinctive, technique, enabling steadier progress to be made and producing a position in which the climber faces the ice in much the same way as he would face the rock, supported by the tips of his feet in both cases. The parallel between ice and rock is made all the closer by the fact that the flexible espadrilles which were used in years gone by, and which necessitated the resistance method (adherence by pulling with the arms and pushing with the feet), have been replaced by boots with rigid, laminated soles, making it possible to stand more securely on the toes on very small holds, sometimes measuring only a few square centimetres.

The 'leading-points' technique demands a good deal of vigour in the muscles of the foot and leg; it is nevertheless more normal than the acrobatic torsion of the ankles – tiresome and a little uncertain, and hampered by the uppers of the boots and the straps of the crampons – which is demanded by the 'all-points' technique.

For my own part, I bought a pair of 'leading-points' crampons as long ago as 1946; I still have them, after a number of climbs, including the north face of the Matterhorn in June 1949, when I used them not only in the initial ice-gully but throughout the climb, the rock being covered with verglas, and the north face of the Eiger in August 1952, when, bad weather having enveloped the face during the first bivouac, I wore them for the whole of the rest of the climb, on the second and third days.

3

4

5

It seems to me that the two leading points might well be provided with serrations like those on the pick of the ice-axe, at least on crampons which are required to 'anchor' well (the Charlet Super-Conta, for example). I also think it would be advantageous if the frame of the crampon was not curved to follow the lateral outline of the boot but was straight, in line with the two leading points, so that these points would drive in better and 'anchor' more firmly.

Crampons with horizontal leading points enable one to use both techniques, the 'leading-points' and the 'flat-footed' or 'all-points', and thus to lessen fatigue by sharing it between the two sets of movements and muscles by adopting whichever technique suits the varying terrain, the consistency of the snow or ice and the fluctuating steepness of the slope.

Above a certain altitude, the leading-points technique will usually be preferred; its special value is that it allows the climber to tackle extremely steep places by the most direct route and in the shortest time, without cutting steps. Nevertheless the training of an ice climber should embrace both methods: the all-points technique is excellent for toughening and suppling the ankles, and will also enable the climber to become acutely and accurately aware of the limits of his ability to keep his balance on ice. At high altitudes this technique will be found useful on slopes up to 40 degrees, and even on steeper ones if the route chosen is zigzag instead of direct, or if long traverses have to be made.

ARTIFICIAL METHODS

Artificial climbing is not usually necessary on ice; however, the shoulder technique is fairly often used for negotiating bergschrunds, cornices and ice walls, and ice-pitons are often employed for running or standing belays, abseiling and short passages of artificial climbing.

Shoulder technique. The procedure is exactly the same as on rock; the leader climbs on a knee of the second who has first securely belayed, then onto his shoulders. The problem is a good deal more complicated if the obstacle to be negotiated is ice: the leader stands on his partner's shoulders without crampons, and cuts steps; if he absolutely must keep his crampons on, the second should protect himself with his rucksack while the leader takes great care that the part of his foot which goes onto the second man's shoulder is between two rows of crampon points.

Piton technique. The long pitons, tubular or with a flat blade, which were formerly used have been advantageously replaced by ice-screws. These are used for belaying on a pitch, belaying between pitches and, if necessary, for artificial climbing; this is rarely necessary on ice, though useful sometimes for negotiating a wall or a bergschrund.

Choose a place where the ice is compact and of an even consistency.

Light solid screws. Do not take a hammer to these. Start the hole with the ice-axe, then put in the screw, turning it by hand; when this becomes difficult, use the hammer or ice-axe as a handle to give leverage.

Tubular screws and stout solid screws. With these there is no need to make a hole with the ice-axe. If you have a hammer with you, give the screw one or two light taps to start it, then proceed as above.

Using crampons on a steep slope. 'All-points' technique with 10-point crampons. Ice-axe in anchor position (1–2–3).

Using crampons on a steep slope. 'Leading-points' technique with 12-point crampons. Ice-axe in adze-head position (4).

MOVING ON SNOW AND ICE

On rock, the climber resorts to artificial climbing only when the resources of free climbing have been exhausted.

On snow and ice, the same rule should be followed: crampons should not be put on automatically because one happens to be on a glacier; nor should one automatically start cutting steps if a slope becomes steeper.

The climber should therefore learn to move without crampons whenever possible. Not only does this make one lighter; direct contact of the foot with the snow, and to some extent with the ice (granular ice), without intermediate equipment, permits the development of a kind of kinship with snow and ice and enables one at the same time to gain an enhanced awareness of balance and to experience a certain pleasure through approaching the limits of what is possible. On the other hand, the condition governing us all is a correct awareness of our limitations; as soon as the climber is in any doubt he must put on his crampons—without, however, taking it into his head that they will do the climbing for him and cut out the difficulties and, more important still, the risks. Using crampons is something which has to be learnt, like skiing, and involves the experience of a new kind of equilibrium.

Moreover, crampon technique—whose primary ingredient is a knowledge of snow and ice and their innumerable varieties, which often change in a short time because of a rise or fall in temperature—must be developed to the highest possible degree. The climber must feel and understand just why his feet are holding, and how securely; and just how far he can go on ten points or the leading points, so as not to start cutting steps before it is really necessary. On the other hand he must be able to foresee and avoid the critical moment at which he gets stuck and feels paralysed, unable to proceed on crampons because the slope is too steep, and powerless to cut steps because he lacks freedom of movement and might endanger his balance. Let us recall that gentle slopes are those up to 25 degrees; medium slopes go from 25 to 40 degrees, steep slopes from 40 to 50 degrees and very steep slopes from 50 degrees upwards. The vital thing, before starting up a slope, is to look at it, study it, pick the best route—which in practice means visualizing it as a sequence of passages—paying attention to the quality of the snow or ice, the steepness of the slope, the temperature and orientation; all of which, be it said, is a source of deep, satisfying pleasure. For example, it will be possible to tackle a slope of 45 degrees, or even more, in perfect safety without crampons, provided the snow is hard and sound, just right, as is sometimes the case in summer (but not all summers), in June, when there is still some winter snow left—or, more likely, spring snow, snow which has been well transformed and is sticking to the under-layer of ice; or in September, when there has been a fall of half-wet, half-powdery snow which has stuck well to the ice. A night frost—not too severe, however—is necessary to produce this condition. The resulting hard snow is still soft enough for a fairly energetic kick to force the front of the boot into the surface of the slope (another reason for using rigid, steel-laminated soles), yet hard enough to support the climber's weight even though, all the way up a steep slope, the actual bearing-surface at every moment is small.

Conversely, there are days when it would be out of the question not to cut steps or use crampons when crossing a small 'throat' covered with gully ice, though the angle of slope may be less than 25 degrees, especially if it has rained on the previous day and frozen hard during the night. The indications given below are therefore no more than a general guide. However, I find it pleasing (and quite apart from my own feelings I think it is reassuring) that it is impossible to reduce the mountains, or even merely the technique of mountaineering on ice, snow and rock, to a methodical programme bristling with columns, figures and co-ordinates. On the other hand, there is, of course, no question of setting out at random and muddling through; we have to think, estimate, understand–which is a way of loving snow and rock–and then to decide on the most logical course of action.

Moving without crampons on deep snow

Deep powder snow. Normal progression, with the ice-axe in the walking-stick position. The amount the legs and feet are lifted will be governed by the depth of the snow; in some cases it will be necessary to press the snow together at each step.

If the boot-sole reaches the underlying layer of hard snow, make the tip of the sole (in a direct ascent), or the edge (on a traverse or a slanting ascent), bite into that layer. On the descent, move cautiously and suit the technique to the nature of the under-layer.

If, on a steep slope, the layer of powder-snow is thin, put on crampons. If it is thick there will be the danger of an avalanche, especially when moving across a slope.

Deep wet snow. This makes for heavy going. It will sometimes be necessary to compress the snow at every step, lifting the feet and legs high, and using the ice-axe in the walking-stick position or shaft position.

On a medium-steep slope, avoid traverses (because of the risk of an avalanche); go up straight; compress the snow at every step to give a solid support; transfer the body-weight gradually from one step to the next; if necessary, get extra help by using the knees and the ice-axe (adze-head or walking-stick position).

On a steep slope, crampons must be used; though on some very sticky kinds of snow it is better not to wear them, because of 'balling-up'.

On deep, very wet snow the danger of an avalanche is great.

Rotten snow. This is usually old snow, often saturated with water after several frostless nights in succession; or it may be fresh snow which has got warmed up during the day and has not been frozen during the night because the temperature, even at high altitudes, has stayed too high. As a result the snow is dangerous, heavy and may avalanche. Avoid traverses; ascend directly, compressing the snow so as to get down to the under-layer, if possible, enabling the tips of the feet to bite into it. Be careful when shifting the weight from one foot to the other.

On the descent it is often best to come down backwards, supporting oneself on the ice-axe (adze-head position) and using great care when transferring the weight from one foot to the other.

Moving without crampons on hard snow

Hard snow slightly softened on the surface. Progress is easy and enjoyable. The ascent can either be direct, pressing down with the front half of the feet, or zigzag, pressing down each foot in turn so as

Left:
Moderately hard snow ('neige à bout de pied', in which only the tips of the feet break through). Ice-axe in walking-stick position.

Below:
On the Col des Nantillons.

Next two pages:
Climbing Mont Blanc: going through the 'Junction'.

Climbing a very steep slope.

to make shallow steps in the snow; the ice-axe will be in the walking-stick, glissading or adze-head position, depending on the steepness of the slope. But great care must be taken, because this species of snow is often very slippery.

If the softening of the surface has gone a little deeper, the feet go in further and the ice-axe is used in the shaft position.

On the descent, according to the degree of the slope, one makes long, gliding steps, with the ice-axe in the walking-stick position; or glissades down (seated, crouching or standing glissade); or comes down on the heels, facing downhill (ice-axe in walking-stick position), on moderately steep slopes; or on the front of the feet (ice-axe in walking-stick or shaft position), facing the slope, on steep slopes.

Hard snow. On the ascent, on a gentle or moderate slope (ice-axe in walking-stick position) or on a steep one (ice-axe in adze-head or shaft position), a single well-directed kick will make the front of the foot penetrate the snow to half-way along the sole. This snow, rather hard but not too much so, is not hard snow with a softened surface but has its own characteristic consistency all the way through. Conditions are ideal for climbing without crampons (so far from helping, they would actually slow you down), even on very steep slopes, and progress is pleasant, very safe, quick and un-fatiguing. On the descent, use the ice-axe in the walking-stick position, face outwards and dig in vigorously with the heels: the toes should be pointing as nearly as possible straight downhill, so that the heel is presented like a cutting edge when it meets and penetrates the surface of the snow-slope.

Brittle snow. This is snow which is crusted on the surface and soft underneath. On the flat (with the ice-axe in the walking-stick position) try to stay on the surface by 'making yourself as light as you can'. Walk lightly, distributing the weight of the body over the whole surface of the sole, and do not swivel the rear foot, otherwise the front of it will go through the crust. The transfer of weight from foot to foot should be made gently.

On a medium slope (ice-axe in walking-stick position) or a steep slope (shaft or adze-head position), break the crust with the tip of the boot without too much force and without pushing the foot too deeply in (the heel should remain outside): the foot should not go right through the crust but should be supported, about halfway along, on the broken edge of the crust; the feet should be kept horizontal and the shift of weight from one to the other should be made gently and delicately. If the crust is weak, try to take long strides and avoid breaking it too much and plunging into the under-layer: the aim is to make holes in the crust without breaking it.

On the descent (ice-axe in walking-stick position), walk boldly, facing downhill, breaking the crust and pushing it in.

On a very steep slope, come down backwards and push the front of the feet vigorously in.

If the snow is very hard, so that the foot cannot penetrate, crampons must be used even on a medium slope.

Granular ice. On gentle and medium slopes, granular ice can be climbed without crampons by taking advantage of the little irregularities of the surface; so can the truly granular ice, with a grain comparable to that of granite, which is occasionally encountered.

Conversely, there are times when, after rain, it is quite hard to cross even the flat part of the Mer de Glace, so slippery does the ice become when it has been washed and polished by the rain.

Moving with crampons on deep snow

If the under-layer supporting the fresh snow (powdery or wet), or the rotten snow, consists of very hard snow or of ice, the boot fails to bite, however hard one kicks with the toe, and crampons must be worn.

If the layer of fresh or rotten snow is thin, a kick will be enough to make the leading points of the crampons 'anchor' in the ice or hard snow of the under-layer; but if it is thick it will have to be cleared away to get at the under-layer.

Moving with crampons on ice

1. *'All-points' or 'flat-footed' technique.* Equipment: ten-point crampons.

On gentle slopes (up to 25 degrees): ice-axe in walking-stick position; direct ascent: feet in normal position, more or less turned out according to the steepness of the slope; oblique ascent, and traversing: uphill foot about horizontal, downhill foot slightly turned out (toe pointing slightly downhill); descent: feet slightly turned out.

On medium slopes (from 25 to 40 degrees): ice-axe mainly in glissading position, but the adze-head and walking-stick positions will be used sometimes; direct or oblique ascent and traversing: uphill foot horizontal, downhill foot slightly turned out; descent: (a) direct descent: feet slightly turned out; (b) oblique descent: the steeper the slope, the more the feet will point in the uphill direction.

On steep slopes (from 40 to 50 degrees): ice-axe in glissading or anchor position; oblique ascent, and traversing: uphill foot horizontal, downhill foot slightly turned out; direct ascent: not feasible; descent: as for oblique ascent; but the ice-axe may also be used in the support or handrail position.

On very steep slopes (over 50 degrees): on the ascent, try to make all the points bite; the slope being so steep, the climber's ankles have insufficient flexion to preserve his balance; hence it is essential to use the ice-axe in the anchor position, not merely as an aid to climbing but for keeping the balance. Be conscious of the moment of imbalance which occurs when the ice-axe is being shifted from one anchor-point to another.

When the steepness of the slope prevents the uphill foot from passing between the slope and the downhill foot, both feet follow parallel lines, without passing each other.

To gain increased balance when shifting the ice-axe from one anchor point to another, get a secure hold with the downhill foot and have the uphill foot about on a level with the calf of the downhill leg, slightly behind it, and pointing slightly downhill.

2. *'Leading-points' technique.* Equipment: twelve-point crampons (with which the 'flat-footed' technique can also be used when desired).

Ascent: the ice-climber goes straight up, facing the slope, whether it be gentle, medium, steep or very steep. As it gets steeper, he stops using the rear points and relies on the four front ones: the two leading horizontal points 'anchor' firmly in the ice; the two semi-vertical points, just behind these, under the front part of the foot, give added support; on slight and medium slopes, the ice-axe is in the walking-stick position; on steep and very steep slopes the crampons are used in the same way but there are different ways of using

Powder snow on ice on the north face of the Matterhorn.

the ice-axe and the arms; in the anchor position the ice-axe is held with both hands (the Austrians like an ice-axe with a sword-knot, through which the lower hand is put).

The anchor position of the ice-axe makes it possible to climb very steep slopes and, in the event of the climber accidentally slipping, enables him to change quickly to the braking position to control and stop his slide. On the other hand, the anchor position is very tiring.

The other positions used yield four points of support, as against the three obtained by the anchor position:

(a) An ice-axe in one hand, an ice-dagger (or, failing this, an ice-piton) in the other; the hands are at chest-height, and the one with the ice-axe can either be half-way along the handle or holding the adze. Another method is to use the ice-axe in the adze-head position.

(b) An ice-axe in one hand and a hammer-ice-axe in the other (the latter hand holds the head of the hammer-ice-axe). The hands, being kept fairly low, level with the haunches, are then able not only to provide balance but also to aid progression. It is perfectly feasible, and indeed pleasant, to use two ice-axes; but it is inadvisable to use two hammer-ice-axes. It goes without saying that the hammer-ice-axe, like the ice-axe, should have proper serrations and that its point must be kept sharp.

When traversing, the ice climber faces the slope, makes a step sideways (for example with the right foot), brings the left level with the right, then makes another step with the right, and so on. The 'flat-footed' technique can also be used.

On the descent, the climber faces the slope and, depending on the terrain and his own preferences and habits, follows one of the three techniques described for the ascent, as far as his hands are concerned. As for the feet, the 'leading-points' technique is more normal, anatomically speaking, than the 'flat-footed', more natural and instinctive, especially on steep slopes; safer and, in practice, the only practical method. Although the 'flat-footed' technique can be carried to considerable lengths on very steep slopes under climbing school conditions, in actual mountaineering at high altitudes the 'leading-points' technique is quicker and also more economical, especially as regards nervous tension; a climber with a good command of it can make his way up with undisturbed balance and an easy mind. But it has its limits and these must be known, so that before reaching the degree of steepness which is too much for any of the climbers on the rope the leader can start cutting steps, for it is when one is standing motionless, supported by the leading points, that fatigue sets in quickly and twice as sharply as usual, and may develop into cramp.

Hard snow. As on ice, there are two techniques: '*Flat-footed*' and '*all-points*' *technique.* The technique for legs and feet remains the same, the difference is in the position of the ice-axe.

Steep slopes (40–50 degrees): ascent: ice-axe in the walking-stick, glissading or adze-head position, depending on the steepness of the slope and the consistency of the snow; traversing: ice-axe in the walking-stick or glissading position; descent: ice-axe in the walking-stick position (pushing the handle in as deep as possible), or the glissading or handrail position.

Very steep slopes (over 50 degrees): ascent and traversing: ice-axe in walking-stick or shaft position; descent: ice-axe in walking-stick position (pushing the handle in as deep as possible), or the anchor, handrail or glissading position; come down facing outwards or sideways, according to the steepness of the slope.

'Forward-points' technique: Use as on ice, except that the points must be well driven into the slope to make sure they 'anchor' well in the hard snow. Beware of snow which, because of orientation and the time of day, has softened slightly on the surface.

On the other hand, the ice-axe holds better, because generally speaking, and regardless of the position used, the point penetrates hard snow more easily than ice. Do not use the anchor position much, the adze-head position is usually preferable.

Crevasses, bergschrunds and cornices

These are obstacles which the mountaineer should approach with caution and make the best use of his technique to overcome.

Crevasses and snow-bridges. In summer, crevasses and snow-bridges are fairly easily detected, whether the crevasses are open or not. In winter it is much more difficult; moreover the snow, not having yet become stabilized, seals the gaps precariously. On skis the bearing surface is greater and the danger less, provided one is not in the axis of the crevasse.

The climber must learn to divine the presence of a crevasse or a snow-bridge. The surface is always faintly concave, dull and flat in colour, and sometimes riddled with little cracks. Well belayed by his companions, the leader moves forward and probes the ground with his ice-axe, advancing with caution. Sometimes it is possible, by moving along the crevasse, to see how thick the bridge is. Suiting your movement to the firmness of the snow and the thickness of the bridge, take a long, light, gliding step forward; if the bridge collapses, throw yourself down at full length, backwards or forwards, and keep hold of your ice-axe. If the bridge is very frail, cross it on all fours with the hands wide apart, or even crawl over so as to distribute the weight of the body over as great an area as possible. Snow-bridges are particularly dangerous after the first snowfalls, and when there has been a temporary return to mild weather.

Open crevasse. If it is in ice, the edges are clear-cut and one jumps over at the narrowest place, choosing the point that offers the best take-off and landing. Land in as relaxed a manner as you can, especially if wearing crampons; if the landing looks unpromising it is better to take them off.

If the crevasse is in snow, move along parallel to it to see whether its lips are overhanging, then, well belayed, go as close to the edge as possible and stamp the snow down with your feet; jump from there, or if the crevasse is very wide go two or three yards back and take a run, holding the ice-axe, as always in jumping crevasses, slightly forward and to one side. The landing should be supple and relaxed.

Bergschrunds. These are crevasses which are close to rock-faces when there is an abrupt change in the incline, at the foot of ice-gullies, for example.

Generally speaking, bergschrunds are of snow; sometimes one has the luck to find them partially filled in with the remains of an avalanche, in which case one gets over them with crampons or by cutting steps.

If a bergschrund is open and overhanging, the loose or unsafe snow must first be cleared from the upper lip to expose the ice or hard snow. Then plan the sequence of moves: if the upper lip consists

Glissading.

Roping down among the séracs.

of hard snow, drive an ice-axe in deep (with the flat of the handle at right-angles to the direction of the slope); if it is ice, put in an ice-screw. Belay to the ice-axe, or to a snap-link on the ice-screw.

Cut a handhold, or two handholds if possible.

Cut two or three steps for the feet.

Go up very smoothly and gradually. If the bergschrund is definitely an overhang, let another climber help you by the shoulder method.

If necessary, put in a second ice-axe or ice-screw when already belayed to the first, or even held by it; then, unless the bergschrund is of exceptional height, you will gain a foothold on the upper lip.

On the descent, if the bergschrunds are without snow-bridges the climber jumps, taking care to land very flexibly. If the landing-place is bad or if the bergschrund is very high or very overhanging, roping down is the only solution.

Cornices. These are snow formations, often of great beauty, which hang over into space, sometimes by as much as 60 feet, as on the Col de la Brenva. They are found on the crests, generally on the lee side in relation to the prevailing wind, but, because of the varying contours of the slopes below the crest, and the eddies of the wind, they are just as likely to occur on the other side and on either side of the same arête. One should always go along a cornice at some distance from its apex and never go beyond the little crack, sometimes a small crevasse, which indicates the point of separation between the arête and the overhanging mass.

On the ascent, at the top of some cols for example, a cornice tops the slope and bars the way. One must then choose the weak point, which is usually at one edge or the other, and, before attacking it, make sure that one can get over. Sometimes it will be better to make a detour instead. In default of any other solution, the climber will have to knock down the part which will not hold or which overhangs too far, and then proceed as for a bergschrund.

Occasions have been known when climbers had to excavate an almost vertical tunnel to get through the cornice.

Glissading. The main thing is not to let go of the ice-axe, without which it is impossible to stop. Secondly, do not bend over so far that the head is lower than the feet. If wearing crampons, take care that they do not catch, as this can cause a violent lurch and an even more violent fall. If this should happen, throw yourself face down-wards and lean with all your weight on the ice-axe in the 'brake' position. If you are coming down without crampons you can brake with the feet as well. It is fairly easy to stop on a snow slope; on an ice slope it is harder, but if you manage to reduce your speed by a substantial amount you will prevent the climber belaying you from receiving a powerful jerk and make it easier to hold you.

Roping down and mushrooms. Roping down on ice, though less common than on rock, is used for descending ice-walls, berg-schrunds too high for jumping, sérac barriers, or very steep slopes of smooth ice. To fix the ropes it is possible to use the rock spurs to be found at the edges of ice-gullies, or the lumps of rock sticking up from snow slopes, provided they are firmly embedded. But sometimes no suitable rock is available, and other means become necessary.

On an ice-slope, the best solution is to put in an ice-screw and run the abseiling rope through it. If you have not got an ice-screw you will have to cut a 'mushroom'. This takes a fairly long time, because a deep channel has to be hollowed out round the 'mushroom' so that the rope or sling does not spring off. When coming down a line of séracs one sometimes finds blocks of ice which nature herself

has fashioned in the mushroom shape; in this case the work is much simpler – all one does is to carve the groove round the block.

On a snow slope, there is a variety of methods. If the expedition you have in mind includes the descent of a high, overhanging bergschrund, like that on Mont Mallet or the Col Maudit, it will be wise to take with you a wooden stake which can be sunk deep into the snow and round which the abseiling rope can be passed. Otherwise it will be necessary to sacrifice an ice-axe – at least if it is not possible, after clearing away the soft snow, to reach the ice or frozen snow underneath and put in a stout ice-screw; this must be sunk vertically into the slope and used with a very long sling so that the pull of the rope cannot tear it out.

If all these procedures are impossible there is nothing for it but to cut a 'mushroom', but while on ice this operation is usually not so much difficult as tiring, on snow it is much trickier. The 'mushroom' must be large, so that the pull of the rope is resisted by a large, consistent mass, which the rope cannot saw through. In the Oisans district, during a long-distance ski-run with the Ecole de Haute Montagne, we were coming down the Mont de Lans glacier when, towards the end, encountering an unusual fracture surrounded by overhanging cornices, we were obliged to rope down and for this purpose had to cut a 'mushroom'. The snow had not yet stabilized, for we were only halfway through the winter; it was February 1943. I had already done some big climbs but, having lived in the mountains for only three years, I was not yet completely familiar with the different qualities of snow; so I greatly admired the speed and precision with which Lucien Amieux and Alexis Simond pointed out the place where the uneven snow was least unreliable and decided how big the 'mushroom' had to be to be sure it would hold.

We hollowed out a channel about 15 inches deep round a 'mushroom' measuring a yard and a half in diameter, and by this means were able to rope down.

Climbing as a team

The mountains have many pleasures to offer us: beauty of landscape, silence, the joy of climbing; but the best of all these is the comradeship of the rope. When the novice has learnt to move safely on rock and ice, the time comes for him to become one of a team. The rope will link him with his companions during the finest and perhaps the hardest moments of his life. His movements, his decisions, his reactions and his reflexes will at times involve everyone else on the rope.

The composition of the team

A rope-team is normally composed of three climbers, but the two-man rope, though less safe, is quicker, and in the mountains safety and rapidity are often closely related: a rope of two climbers may be able to avoid a dangerous bivouac which a three-man rope, moving more slowly, would be forced to make. A happy solution is often the combination of two ropes of two climbers, which gives speed with safety.

Safety does not depend only on the number of participants, however, but on their competence. A rope of two, made up of one strong and one weak member, is less safe than a rope of three made up of two strong and one weak, but safer than a rope of three comprising one strong and two weak members. If a weak member falls into a crevasse, particularly if he happens to be at the end of the rope, there is a risk that he will drag with him the second weak member placed in the middle, which means that the strong one will have to hold two men instead of one. Personally, I do not like having two novices with me, but if I do, I rope up in tandem: that is to say, I attach myself to the middle of the rope and each of my companions attaches himself to an end; thus I can hold them individually, and can anticipate a fall and check it at its start. One 'feels' many things through a rope, even if an angle of rock is hiding the climber in action; one can tell whether his progress is more or less steady, one can sense his hesitations, one can tell if he is about to stumble, or if he is anxious or getting tired.

It is important to keep up an even pace throughout the climb. One climbs a mountain for pleasure, not to establish a speed record. In the course of the ascent or on the summit, it is always pleasant to stop for a while and look around, but in order to be able to do this with an easy mind one must keep to a timetable which in its turn depends essentially on conditions on the mountain.

The distance at which climbers are roped one from the other depends on the length and difficulty of each pitch. One should always rope up a little longer than the distance between each stance and the next so as to allow the leader some slack as he makes his last pull up, and enable him to belay comfortably. Whether the climbers are moving together or one at a time, the rope should always be fairly taut so that it does not catch, wedge, loosen stones or get caught up in the legs of one of the climbers and throw him off balance; also so that a slip can be checked before it has gained too much momentum.

On easy terrain, the members of the rope move simultaneously,

Going over the Dômes de Miage.

153

very close together, four or five coils of rope in the hand. As each man climbs, he should think of his companions and watch them so as to be ready to pay out the rope if needed. A climber who has just slowed down to get over a tricky patch should not resume his former faster rhythm until his companions, either in front or behind him, have also negotiated it, as a jerk on the rope might throw them off balance just at this difficult moment. On a glacier, the coils are held in the down-slope hand, the up-slope hand holding the ice-axe.

On difficult terrain, each climber moves in his turn, belayed by his companions. If, during part of the ascent, the going gets easier, instead of keeping several coils of rope in the hand, which is an encumbrance, it is better to wind them round the chest, not forgetting to hold them fast by a firm knot on the waist loop.

BELAYING

At the beginning of this book it was stated that before tackling a pitch–any pitch whatsoever–the climber should firmly discount his love of the mountains, his passion for climbing, his eagerness to achieve such-and-such an ascent, and should calculate, with ice-cold clarity, the exact ratio between, on the one hand, the difficulty of the pitch, estimated as accurately as possible after careful study; and, on the other hand, his technique and his physical and psychological strength, also estimated as accurately as possible at that moment.

This ratio, *difficulty of pitch/means at climber's disposal*, generates the decision.

In the ensuing passage of climbing, however, various things can go wrong and cause a climber to lose his hold and fall. Consequently the climber who is belaying, whether he be the leader or the No. 2, must, before his companion starts climbing, ask himself further questions which are corollaries of the first. He must force his imagination to perform the unpleasant task of picturing all the ways in which his companion might lose his hold, and calculate accurately the ratio between:

1. Potential loss of hold, followed by a fall or not, as the case may be, the direction and speed of any such fall, determined by the position of the climber on the wall, the steepness of the latter; the route, direct or sinuous, being followed; the intermediate belaying points (pitons, slings), etc.; and:

2. Potential means for countering loss of hold (and subsequent fall, if any), i.e. belaying station (large or small ledge, level or sloping, and so forth), possibility or otherwise of the belayer being self-belayed, the belaying of the climber in action to a bollard, chockstone, piton, ice-axe or his companion's shoulder or haunches, the climber's ease or difficulty of movement, etc.

This ratio, *loss of hold (perhaps causing fall)/means of belaying*, generates the required tactics.

If it was impossible to lose one's hold when climbing there would never be any need of a belay. Since this is not the case, belaying is essential. But belaying is at once an appreciation of the situation, a responsibility, a difficult technique in which rapidity of execution is fundamental; and, above all, it is preparation. Never, at any time, rely on luck or improvization.

Development of the technique of belaying. In the last fifteen years there have been many changes in the technique of belaying, both as regards the belaying of the leader by the second and vice versa.

1

These changes followed quickly on the adoption of nylon as the material for ropes; they have sprung from studies made by the Americans and by certain European mountaineers, notably Dr Avcin.

Formerly, in the case of the leader falling, there were four possibilities.

The second would check the rope, which then usually broke under the sudden strain (Professor Dodéro's investigations, as we saw in the chapter on ropes, have shown how little real strength there is in ropes, particularly those made of natural fibres).

The second would check the rope and the rope would hold (being a very strong one, or, for the sake of argument, a steel cable); the fall was arrested but the leader was killed nevertheless. In many cases the lethal factor is not the fall itself but the sudden extreme strain on the faller's body when the fall is abruptly checked.

The second was unable to check the rope, was torn from his footing and fell with the leader.

Both men came through unscathed, thanks to a combination of braking effects: friction of both the climber and the rope against the rock, snow or ice; friction of the rope in the belaying snap-links; retarding effect of snap-links being torn out one after another.

In fact, much of the force involved in a fall was absorbed by this retarding effect and these sources of friction, which made it possible for the second man and the rope between them to support the leader and ensured that the leader's fall was largely deadened in successive stages, so that he was little the worse, not having been subjected to the violent impact of a sudden, complete check.

As an instance, here is an extract from the account of the ascent of the north face of the Grandes Jorasses, a climb I did with my friend Edouard Frendo in 1945:

'Towards the middle of the afternoon we arrived under the great step at a height of about 13,000 feet. Once again we had to exert ourselves to the utmost. After an ice couloir and a triangular patch of snow we were stopped by a chimney composed of friable rock. Frendo, more accustomed to bad rock than I, made the first attempt. He traversed twelve feet to my right, then started up the chimney. He drove in a piton, which looked as though it would not hold. At last he was almost at the top, attempting to get a position above a great jammed block which formed an overhang fifty feet above my head. For a moment he hesitated, then he made his decisive move. Just at the moment of achievement I saw him lurch backwards with the block in his arms. His fall lasted the space of a lightning flash, yet to me it all seemed to be happening very slowly. At such moments brain and action are amazingly swift and incisive. As soon as I saw him go I drew in the rope between us very quickly, so as to limit the length of his fall. Then, when he passed my level a little to the right – the piton had not held – I said to myself: "Now I mustn't pull in the rope between us any more, or it will go slipping through my fingers and I shan't be able to hold him." Very quickly I slid the rope round a little leaf of rock in front of me, then took some of the slack in my right hand to soften the shock and so that the rope would not break from too abrupt a jerk on contact with the leaf. Everything held. Frendo came to rest about thirty feet below.' (From *Starlight and Storm* by Gaston Rébuffat, translated by Wilfred Noyce and the Rt Hon. Lord Hunt, published by Kaye & Ward, 1968.)

If I analyse my spontaneous reactions in the moment of emergency, two of them stand out in my mind: as soon as I saw that Frendo

The Walker Spur on the north face of the Grandes Jorasses (1).

A long stride, belayed from above, to effect the transition between the Aiguillette d'Argentières and the Petite Aiguillette (2).

2

was falling I took up some of the slack between us so as to reduce the distance of his fall; and I followed this by taking some slack in my right hand to neutralize the impact and prevent the rope snapping through being too suddenly checked.

I may add that, even today, I remember the terrific jolt that ran through my right hand, fore-arm, upper arm and shoulder and all down my right side and made me crouch slightly with my right thigh and leg. If I had not been holding on securely with my left hand, this tug would no doubt have overturned me.

I had in fact executed instinctively, on that day in 1945, two movements which were not described and recommended in any handbook and had never been taught in the guides' course at the Ecole Nationale d'Alpinisme. These movements had saved the lives of Frendo and myself, and the second of them was in effect an embryonic form of the running belay.

In 1959, in *Les Alpes*, the journal of the Club Alpin Suisse, Dr Avcin published a very interesting article on ropes and 'assurance dynamique', the running belay – the belay in which the belaying rope is not suddenly checked but, on the contrary, is allowed to run under control for a certain distance, progressively slowing down and finally coming to a stop. 'I have had an opportunity [wrote Dr Avcin] of making a thorough study of the running belay at the climbing school in Washington. Every member of the Potomac Appalachian Trail Club, whether man or woman, has to master this technique before being allowed to ascend a rock-face. For convenience, training is carried out on a tall, strong tree. A screw snap-link is fixed halfway up the trunk. The belaying rope goes from the individual executing the belay to this snap-link, and from there to a concrete block which weighs about 155 lb and is nicknamed 'Oscar'. The beginner makes his first belay from a sitting position on the ground, with his outstretched legs pushing against a log. This gives a considerable active length of rope. When the pupil has had a little practice and has got the hang of the method he climbs up to a fork in the branches and belays from there, sitting on a little bench, having first, of course, been roped up for safety. So the length of rope in action is rather less, and the help it provides is thus diminished.

'With the help of a portable power-driven windlass, Oscar is hoisted to whatever height is desired; lower than the snap-link at first, and subsequently above it. A release device, worked by a string on the ground, causes Oscar, who is suspended on the belaying rope, to fall. The belaying rope is in position round the haunches of the individual making the belay.

'During training, the haunches are protected by a broad band of leather (about 20 ins wide) and a leather glove is worn on the belaying hand. Belaying is practised on both sides, i.e. with either hand. The operation is rendered more difficult by the fact that repeated falls make the nylon rope very smooth.

'If the student holds the rope too tight, he is simply lifted off the ground. To prevent this, he is fastened from behind to a stake. By handling the moving rope he learns how best to balance the two opposing forces, the forward and backward pull. Equilibrium is reached when Oscar is not touching the ground. This manoeuvre is comparatively easy to carry out when one is sitting on the ground; it is harder when one is up in the tree and Oscar falls from somewhere above the snap-link, providing the equivalent of a thoroughgoing fall in actual climbing. The necessary resistance then has to be provided by the friction of the rope on the leather, and almost nothing by the short segment of rope actively in play.

Ascent of the Pilier Bonatti on the Drus. The pitch shown here consists of the slabs and dièdre (dihedral) above the ledge which was the site of Bonatti's fifth bivouac.

Leader making a shoulder-belay to support the second (1).

Second climber using a running belay to support the leader, on ice. The position of the arms is reversed according to whether an ice-screw has, or has not, been put in at this level, to belay to. In either case, the second is self-belayed to another ice-screw (2–3).

1

'Such training is extremely useful and conveys a great deal. One learns in a truly spectacular fashion how little chance there is of arresting a direct fall by the old, conventional method, and one forms an estimate of the powerful forces which are exerted *via* the rope and have to be brought under control. One realizes that falls originating from a point above the man belaying can rarely be held by means of belaying round the body alone, even if the man belaying is himself supported by a relay piton. Only the combination of piton technique and the running belay is adequate for reliable belaying. I need hardly stress that the method must be practised until belaying becomes automatic, like a conditioned reflex.'

Dr Avcin had previously carried out experiments in belaying on snow. He writes as follows:

'In order finally to convince myself of the inadequacy of the methods commonly used on snow, I undertook some thorough-going trials in the Julian Alps. Tests were made on an icy, very steep slope ending in a slope of soft snow. The hefty fellow subjecting himself to the fall was wearing a smooth rubberized storm suit. He was belayed by one of our strongest men, with a long experience of winter climbing. The latter began by trying the classical method of belaying round the shoulder, standing in steps as big as bath-tubs and fastened to an ice-axe driven into the snow. Despite being mentally prepared and having the best conditions for belaying he was pulled off every time, and his ice-axe with him, and came sliding down. The causes were that the point of application was too high and that the rope was held rigidly, so that the force was too sudden, too much of a jerk. Everyone else had the same experience. We then went over to the running belay. After a few trials I (and, after me, all the other participants in the course) succeeded in controlling any fall whatsoever, almost with one hand alone; the falls moreover were deliberately contrived to be as violent as possible. We found that if a number of trials were to be made it was best to protect with a leather glove the hand used as a brake on the rope. From that time on, the running belay was used in every course of climbing instruction in Slovenia.

'Having been through these two bouts of training, one on snow in the Alps and the other on the 'tree rock' in Washington, I have conceived a horror of every form of static belaying. A shiver goes down my spine at the thought of the various possible risks whenever I see any kind of belay other than the dynamic belay being used on a difficult pitch. I consider the static belay to be permissible only when carried out from above, with the rope already in tension.'

There are thus two distinct forms of belay: the traditional, or static, belay, in which the leader belays the second; and the dynamic or running belay, in which the second belays the leader. However, before dealing with the belay from a stance, we must emphasize the importance of intermediate belaying between stances.

Belaying between stances

In a great many falls, the factor which saved the team, or which prevented a member of it from being in a tricky position after losing his hold, was the intermediate points of support. These are usually pitons or ice-screws put in at intervals, especially in traverses, when they have the advantage of making pendulums unnecessary. However, line slings, or webbing slings which are decidedly superior to line, are preferable to pitons. For this reason, every climber should have with him ten or a dozen webbing slings and put them in position as often as possible. Driving a piton in is

slow and tiring and getting it out is even more so; putting a sling in place and subsequently retrieving it takes very little time and no energy; and the suppleness and elasticity of webbing can be important factors in the event of a fall, besides allowing the ropes to run better in the snap-links.

A webbing sling can be put over a rock bollard, including a bollard sticking up out of an ice-slope. The webbing's flat surface gives it better adherence than line, so that it is less likely to slip off. It can also be passed through two holes in the rock, side by side, with a tunnel connecting them; or round a chockstone; or through a piton or round a wedge. It can even be put on a projecting shoulder of rock without a hollow behind it – at least on granite, the grain of which digs into the texture of the webbing; a sling in this position will hold provided the climber is below it and exerts a downward pull; but the security it provides is comparatively slight, since the sling will come off as soon as the climber has gone past it. Moreover, a webbing sling round a rock bollard, with the climber below it, can also be made to come off by the rope's varying movements and direction.

This technique – belaying by means of a webbing sling on a protruding rock – is still not much used. But in view of its great advantages – the ease and quickness with which it can be placed, the considerable help it gives in the event of a fall, the shock-absorption caused by its stretching and by friction against the rock – and in spite of its disadvantages, it deserves to be more widely adopted. As has been pointed out, there are at present two grades of webbing; it is advisable to use the stronger one (1 in wide, 3,525 lb b.s.), the lighter (0·6 in wide, 1,540 lb b.s.) being used only when the stronger one would be too thick to go into a very narrow gap between the protuberant rock and the wall.

It is well to stress the importance of security in the course of a belay, whether it be obtained by slings or pitons; the higher the leader goes above the second climber, the greater the importance becomes. Consider these two examples, in which it is assumed that the same pair of climbers, with the same ropes, is involved:

In the first example, a climber sets out from the stance, climbs 15 feet, and falls; the distance through which he falls will be 30 feet.

In the second example, a climber sets out from the stance, climbs 60 feet and puts in a piton; at 75 feet he falls. Here again, the length of the fall will be 30 feet. The two cases may look similar, but in fact they are nothing of the kind. Without going into details, the strain placed on the rope in the second case will be only one-fifth of that in the first, since the shock-absorbing effect will be distributed over a length of rope five times as great.

None of this reduces the value of the running belay, which works by artificially increasing the dynamic strength of a rope and reducing the impact of a fall.

On the other hand, if the leader had not provided himself with an extra belay at 60 feet, he would have fallen 150 feet.

The leader belaying the second climber

The traditional, static belay is still valid for this purpose. The main thing to be remembered is that the rope must be continuously in tension, so that if the second slips he will not fall; the fall is arrested almost before it has begun. The most that can happen to him is to lose a small amount of height, owing to the rope stretching. Moreover, even when the leader is unable to see the second he can feel a great deal through the medium of the rope, and on anticipating a

possible slip on the part of the No. 2 he will be able to belay tighter for a moment.

To belay effectively, the leader should be vertically above the second, so that if the latter does come off the rock face he will not swing. If the pitch has to be tackled slant-wise, the leader will in many cases be able to provide two or three belaying-points to one side or the other of the line of advance, so as to belay the second as immediately overhead as possible. If he has not enough freedom of movement to do this, the leader will set up a belaying point where he is, or, for preference, higher up, to his right or left, so as to achieve the same result.

If the team is climbing with two ropes the matter is simple enough: one rope follows the actual path of the climb, the other (either because the leader does not put it through the snap-links, or because he takes it out of them by pulling it up after him, the second having unfastened it from himself, and then throws it down for the second to fasten it on again) belays the second man direct. The problem varies according to the length of the traverse and especially according to how far it may be from the stance; it may be as little as 10 feet from one stance, or as much as 50 feet.

Even if the traverse is long, but situated a good way below the belaying point, the pendulum effect will be much diminished by the rope affording a direct belay, bypassing the snap-links.

Conversely, if the traverse is long but is only 6 or 9 feet below the belaying point (an example is the traverse which terminates the first pitch on the 'directissime', the 'super-direct' ascent, of the Scoiatoli on the Torre Grande d'Averan), belaying becomes much harder; indeed, a passage of this sort should not really be attempted at all except by climbers fully capable of climbing safely without being directly belayed. There are nevertheless several possibilities.

The leader can go as high as possible above the stance and put one of the ropes through a belaying point high up, vertically above the second if this can be managed.

Alternatively, the second climber can put one of his two ropes through a sling (or a ring-piton) which he puts in position at the start of the traverse; and as the second executes the traverse, the leader pays out one of the ropes and draws in the other; the second is thus belayed horizontally in both directions throughout the traverse. At the end of the traverse, or even of the whole pitch, he disconnects from himself the rope which is through the sling, pulls it in and, when he has got it out of the sling, recovers it and attaches it to himself again.

Difficult traverses are usually encountered in the course of climbs which are themselves difficult, so that the climbers are double-roped. If, however, for some reason or other, a difficult traverse has to be executed when they are only single-roped, the leader must make sure that he has a sufficient number of pitons or slings to enable the second man to execute the traverse; he will then also have to decide whether – depending on the length of the traverse and particularly on its distance from the stance – it is preferable to leave the rope in the snap-links or, on the contrary, to take it out of them and lower it to the second man so as to effect a direct belay; in which case the second will help himself along by means of the snap-links, or the snap-links and slings, left in place by the leader.

For the belay itself there are two possible methods. Either the leader gives a direct shoulder-belay, or a belay to some fixed point can be used: a line or webbing sling, a rock bollard, a 'tunnel' between two holes (as already described), a chockstone, or a piton.

Direct shoulder-belay. This is sound practice if, and only if, the leader (the man belaying) is completely and unconditionally certain of his ability (a) to hold the second climber in the event of a slip, and then (b) to help him by pulling on the rope.

If both these conditions are satisfied, this method at once gives the most immediate support at the moment when the slip occurs, and the most immediate help thereafter. But it does demand that the leader be quite sure of himself: he must be securely positioned and also certain that he possesses adequate strength. The technique is the one fairly frequently used by guides, and has never proved unsatisfactory. It is true that for a guide it becomes a habit, an automatic reflex, to keep the rope continuously taut, which enables him to sense any hesitation on the part of the second and instantly to check a slip and prevent it from developing further. Moreover the guide, having taken up a firm position, can then, if necessary, proceed to pull the second man up to get him over the difficult place. To pull a man up (a weight of, say, 180 lb, plus a certain amount to allow for friction) is not easy; nor, on the other hand, is it as hard as people think. The exertion, after all, is, though differently applied, about the same as that required for swarming up a rope. The great thing, as in so many other matters, is decision: act fast, so as to avoid getting too tired, and make sure at the outset that you are firmly based on your feet and legs.

My reason for explaining the shoulder-belay at such length is that it is the method often used by guides, and that amateurs are astonished by it. The essential condition is never to be taken by surprise, otherwise the result may be catastrophic. Therefore, if the method is employed by anyone without much experience, it is absolutely necessary that the leader should first belay himself (though in these circumstances it is really preferable, because safer, for the second man also to belay to a sling).

Position for the shoulder-belay. The man belaying should place himself turned slightly to one side, wedged in a secure position and well buttressed by his legs and feet. The rope coming up from the second climber should pass along the leader's outer leg, under his outer arm and over his inner shoulder (i.e. the shoulder nearest to the rock). Even if the platform is wide and deep the man belaying should be fairly close to its outer edge, so that the rope is parallel to his outer leg. If he were to station himself at the inner edge of a deep platform, the rope, so far from being parallel to his outer leg, would then bear on the upper part of his body alone and would acutely jeopardize his balance. Hence the necessity for his being at the edge of the platform in order to belay effectively. On the other hand, it is obvious that the leader must in no circumstances lean outwards towards the second in order to point out a hold or explain something or other to him; he must remain upright where he is stationed.

Instead of belaying round the shoulder, as indicated here, it is also possible to belay with the rope crossed, either once or twice.

Indirect belay. This is the best solution. It is effected by means of a line or webbing sling placed round a protruding rock, a leaf of rock, a large block or chockstone, or through a 'tunnel' between two holes in the rock; or by pitons or wedges.

Choice of means. The important thing is that, in order to avoid a double manoeuvre and hence a loss of time, the leader should choose a means of belaying which will not only belay the second man but also serve to belay the leader himself when, having been joined by the second, he starts ascending again.

In making his choice, therefore, the leader will think of his

Pendulum traverse, above the passage of artificial climbing on the south face of the Clocher du Portalet (1).

Running belay on rock (2).

2

being belayed in turn by the second (a much more complicated belay than when the second is belayed by the leader). A rock bollard is the means most often used; but the safest is a 'tunnel' (or, alternatively, pitons or wedges) because it is then physically impossible for the sling to slip off, however unpredictable (as they sometimes are) the movements of the rope in the event of a fall; moreover this kind of anchor-point is better than a bollard for taking a load which may come on it at any angle.

The *sling*, whether of rope or webbing, must always fulfil the following requirements:

It must be at least as strong as the belay rope. To ensure this it will often be necessary to use two or three separate slings of equal length, parallel but independant, not a single long sling doubled or trebled; or else the long sling must be knotted in two places or three, making it equivalent to two or three shorter, independent slings.

The sling must be of adequate length. It must not just go round a bollard or leaf, or behind a block or through a tunnel, with nothing left over; it must hang down.

If the bollard, hole or block has cutting edges, they must be chipped off and smoothed with the hammer. The sling can also be protected by putting a crumpled handkerchief or a piece of paper at the vital spot between it and the rock.

Ideally, the belaying point should be level with the face of the belayer; failing this, it should be a little higher rather than lower, at least when the leader is belaying the second.

Finally, if a single belaying point gives too little security or covers too narrow an angle of fall (a fall in one direction only, for example), two points should be used. If the climbers have no sling with them, a sling can be made with the climbing rope (the appropriate knot is the bowline or the 'queue de vache'). However, this deducts several yards from the amount of rope available for climbing with, and restricts freedom of manoeuvre.

Chockstones. These are usually blocks wedged in a crack or a chimney; they should always be examined to make sure that traction cannot make them pivot or come away. Sometimes a similar formation is found where very large blocks lie against one another at different angles, leaving spaces between their points of contact. And sometimes enormous blocks are found standing on a platform, leaning against the rock face and wedged into it.

'Tunnels'. In most cases, these have been hollowed out by erosion eating away soft material from the hard rock surrounding it. Obviously, the two holes connected by the tunnel must not be so far apart that the sling cannot be put through them. Sometimes it will be found that a crack is closed on the surface for a short distance, but hollow inside. Again, little rock-pillars may be encountered, behind which a sling can be threaded.

Bollards, spikes, leaves. Check these for strength. The sling must not go tightly round them like a crown but should go down deep into the gap between the protruding rock and the wall, and come down low on the downhill side of the protuberance, so that there is no danger of its either slipping over the top or breaking.

Pitons, wedges. If no other possibility presents itself it will be necessary to put in a piton, or else to adopt the ingenious British technique (which, however, demands much experience) of inserting a metal or plastic wedge (or a bolt), of suitable size, in a crack.

In some positions, the piton should be 'prolonged' by having a sling attached to it.

Using the belaying point. The man belaying first belays himself to

Belaying is indispensable, admittedly; but the sense of balance is even more so! (1)

Belaying to a sling and snap-link on a rock bollard (2).

Belaying to a piton (3).

the belaying point by fixing his rope (with a bowline or a figure-of-eight knot) to a snap-hook attached to the sling.

When the leader is belaying the second, he can either use a shoulder-belay, as indicated above, unless he is self-belayed; or he can belay to the sling. To do this, he puts the climbing rope through a second snap-hook attached to the sling and, holding the rope in both hands, draws it up through the snap-link as the second man climbs towards him; one hand comes up with the part of the rope coming from below, the other hand comes down with the rope issuing from the snap-link and approaches the first hand; it is recommended to make a turn of the rope round the downhill hand, the one holding the rope as it comes out of the snap-link.

Every time an arm's length of rope is gained, the belayer holds both ropes for a moment with the downhill hand, giving himself just time to make a fresh turn of the rope round the uphill hand.

Take care to keep the rope in tension all the time.

If he requires to help the second, the leader buttresses himself with his feet and legs as for the shoulder-belay (but of course without putting the rope over his shoulder) and with his downhill hand pulls powerfully on the rope coming from the second, reinforcing the pull with a movement of his whole body and taking up the slack progressively with his uphill hand. If he is unable to help the second sufficiently, that is to say if he cannot hold and raise him, he should resort to the technique of the self-tightening knot (the Prusik or one of the other knots of this class). However, on very difficult pitches the climbers will be using not the single but the double rope, in which case the best method is to arrest one of the ropes (by a bowline on a third snap-link) thus converting it into a fixed rope by which the second can hold on and pull himself up (alternatively, an étrier with a self-tightening knot can be put on this fixed rope, while the leader energetically pulls on the other rope so as to help the second with as much traction as he is capable of exerting).

For more complicated manoeuvres, which are fortunately seldom needed, under big overhangs, in other words in extreme cases which lie outside the scope of this work, the reader should consult Gianni Mazenga's book, *Sécurité en paroi* (Safety on the Rockface).

Second man belaying the leader

This is not just a question of supporting a suspended weight but of slowing-down and arresting a fall, which means resisting a large, very violent impact; the difference between the two situations being the considerable force which the weight acquires while falling.

A fall is in fact a source of energy, and controlling and arresting the fall implies the problem of absorbing that energy; for it must not be imagined that merely bringing the fall to a stop is enough to preserve the faller from harm; it must not be forgotten that in many cases what kills the faller is not the fall itself but the abrupt, almost instantaneous manner in which he is halted. To convince oneself that this is so one has only to picture to oneself a falling body supported on a rope as strong as a steel cable: the cessation of movement would be so sudden that the human body, despite its amazing potentialities, would be incapable of surviving it, whereas it can withstand a fall from a considerable height provided the cessation takes place more gradually. 'In purely static belaying,' writes Dr Avcin, 'the braking process takes place very quickly, too quickly. In one-tenth of a second – almost instantaneously after the rope has completely tightened – the fall is halted, unless the climber

2

3

163

It has been my good fortune to make over 1,000 ascents, in many different massifs; and while equipment has played its part, my principal ally is the sense of balance. Many of these ascents were difficult, some were very difficult. Nevertheless, and in spite of my still increasing experience, the thought often comes to me that 'we are only tiny human creatures in the immensity of the mountains'.

has collided with rocks on the way down. It is this very high speed of braking which, in the most severe falls, makes the forces involved so irresistibly great.'

The goal to be attained is therefore twofold: the rope must not break, and the check must not be too brutal. The reasons why falls were in many cases not fatal are these: (a) the strength and elasticity of the rope, or, more precisely, its shock-absorbing potential, neutralizing the kinetic energy of the falling body by transforming it into heat-energy through deformation of the rope, a further neutralizing factor being contributed by the body of the faller; (b) all the friction caused by the rope rubbing on the rock and through the snap-links; (c) friction between the rock and the falling climber, and even (however small) between him and the air.

These considerations were what prompted the American mountaineer and physicist Wexler to conceive the idea that by increasing these various frictions it would be possible to bring a fall under control and halt it safely.

In practical terms, this boils down to 'assurance dynamique', the running belay. Before explaining how this works, it is necessary to recapitulate the improvements which have been made in other aspects, namely: the development of nylon ropes, which are stronger and, above all, more elastic, that is to say they stretch, becoming longer more readily than ropes of natural fibres; the complete shoulder-harness, which distributes and absorbs the shock more effectively than roping-up to the waist or chest only; and the helmet, protecting the head during a fall.

The running belay. The man belaying must take the preliminary precaution of unrolling his sleeves and doing them up at the wrist, if he has so far been climbing with bare arms; he must wear gloves.

He must, of course, be self-belayed.

He must keep his eyes fixed on the leader as the leader climbs; if the leader is out of sight, the second man must be doubly attentive to the upward movement of the rope. It is vital for the second to sense, through the rope, what the leader is doing.

Sometimes the leader is able to realize that he is going to have a fall. At this moment it is better for him to do something rather than remain inactive: he should make a jump, or let himself slide down the rock-face towards a piton, or whatever else is apposite, and of course he should warn the man belaying him. But in most cases the fall is unseen. The time-lag, the moment of surprise undergone by the belayer, must be reduced as far as humanly possible. Naturally, the belayer should not be constantly expecting the leader to fall, otherwise mountaineering would be a nightmare. But he must be continually on the alert, ready to take action, and must therefore never allow his attention to stray, even momentarily.

If the belayer is an experienced climber, and provided he is in good form at the time, with all his reflexes sharp, he can very quickly pull on the rope so as to reduce the distance through which the leader will be carried by the fall. This does not apply to a free fall but only to a sliding fall–which takes place very quickly, it is true, but not *as* quickly. The remedy is one which needs a very clear head and excellent reflexes, but may be extremely beneficial.

Position to be adopted by the belayer. Belaying over the shoulder is out of the question: the amount of friction between rope and body would be reduced too much, freedom of manoeuvre would be too small, the point of application of the force would be located too high and the leverage too great, upsetting the belayer's balance.

The belayer must pass the rope behind him, against his back:

165

either at waist level, above his self-belay, especially in free climbing (without pitons), so that when the leader's fall has come to rest the second can withstand the traction coming from below; or the rope should be at the level of his haunches – or under his buttocks, at the junction of the buttocks and the thighs – if he foresees that strong pitons or slings, used intermediately within the pitch, will cause the pull to come from above.

On one side, the rope is held by the guiding hand, the job of which is simply to direct the rope, without trying to check it; the hand which does this is the one which is nearest the leader, who is climbing. On the other side, the rope is held by the controlling hand; a twist of the rope is made round this hand and wrist. For extra strength, this hand should be supported on the thigh, and the elbow should be held against the chest.

The leader should make a belay before the rope becomes fully extended, so that the second will still have some slack at his disposal to pay out when required. Every case is different and must be treated on its merits, but a convenient reckoning is that the length of spare rope should be about one-fifth of the total fall.

The running belay, which is the best method when the second is belaying the leader, runs directly counter to the fear-reflex, which automatically prompts the belayer to check the rope and contract his muscles to hold the faller. The technique must be learnt in training before applied in actual climbing; when it has been carefully studied it becomes a reflex action, based ultimately on cool, intelligent thinking.

The Sticht-Salewa brake-plate. As was logically to be expected, mountaineers and manufacturers have sought to invent a device rendering it possible to effect a running belay mechanically – more easily, if possible, and in any case with less apprehension, than by the manual technique indicated above.

To this end, Sticht-Salewa has brought out a brake-plate which, in a way, stands in the same relation to the running belay as does the descendeur to abseiling (all the more so in that abseiling can be regarded, to some extent, as a controlled fall). This plate can be used either as a descendeur in abseiling, or as a means of checking the rope when the second climber is being belayed by the leader. But its primary purpose is to facilitate the execution of a running belay, and this it achieves because of the way it enables the two hands to co-operate, so that the necessary movements are smooth and comfortable, the requisite reflex action is easily acquired, and the rope runs under better control. Minor falls, in which the belaying equipment is not subjected to a sudden violent strain, do not cause the rope to run. The hand stopping or braking the rope is always the one which comes 'after' the brake-plate. When the pull exceeds 200/250 kilos (from 440 to 550 lb), the rope automatically starts running. The brake-plate is automatically pulled up against the snap-link and acts as a brake until the rope is brought to a complete stop, also automatically.

Though the advantages of the brake-plate are considerable, care must be taken when using it that the rope does not kink and cause a check. Another drawback is that the rope soon suffers from 'fatigue' because all the energy that the plate causes to be absorbed is converted into heat, and this heat is confined to a small area – the plate itself and part of the snap-link, which become intensely hot and, by heating the rope, impair its elasticity to some extent. An abrupt, heavy fall, imposing great tension on the rope, forces the plate sharply against the snap-link; the rope rapidly becomes

Using the Sticht-Salewa brake-plate. Traction or a fall brings the two parts of the rope into a straight line with each other. The 'braking hand' instinctively holds the rope; thus the plate is pulled against the snap-link, exerting a braking action on the rope. When double-roping, use two snap-links, and position them so that the slots in the plate are in line with the long axes of the snap-links. When putting the ropes through, take care not to twist them, as this would cause kinking.

fatigued because of the short, acute in-and-out bend to which it is subjected at this point. It is therefore essential that the rope or ropes should be in excellent condition at the start, that they are thick enough and, naturally, that they have no kinks.

Again, ill-luck may have it that, just when the snap-link is brought forcibly into play, it is lying crossways, perhaps even with the strain coming directly on its weakest part, the opening side.

All the same, the brake-plate is undoubtedly an attractive accessory, and it is likely that new versions of it will be developed, eliminating these drawbacks.

Belaying on snow and ice. The foregoing principles and advice hold good; it is just a matter of adapting them to snow and ice.

None the less, I think it worth while to glance quickly at possible causes of accidents and the corresponding safety-measures.

Through the activities of climbing schools, rock has become a familiar element to the climber, even when he is on a kind of rock on which he has had little practice. On granite, limestone, gneiss and so on the position of the body is much the same and the hands always have something to grasp; they contribute constantly to maintaining balance. Movement on rock is climbing, in the ordinary sense of the term.

Movement on snow and ice rarely consists of climbing but, rather, of walking over more-or-less steep ground. The body-weight describes a continuous swinging movement from foot to foot, up or down the slope as the case may be. There is nothing for the hands to grasp, except when handholds are cut with the ice-axe or ice-pitons or screws are put in. Indeed, one hand is holding the ice-axe, which is mostly used for supporting, not pulling.

Thus, in addition to the fact that, to the climber, snow and ice are alien substances, compared with rock, the position of balance is different and is achieved differently.

Moreover, whereas rock remains unaltered throughout the day (except that parts of it may be wet or covered with verglas or snow), snow and ice can change in appearance, consistency, adhesion to the slope and firmness, a number of times in the course of a single day, and even at intervals of a few minutes. Some of the factors determining these changes are the time of night or day; the orientation of the slope or of different parts of it; sunshine direct or slanting, or strong or weak; clouds briefly blanketing the sun; sudden winds which may be warm, cold or icy; the presence of rock close to the surface of the snow or ice deep below it, or the presence of ice close to the surface of the snow or deep below it; the degree to which the snow has or has not been compacted, or swept by snow-streams or avalanches, in small ice-gullies for example, or washed by rain or darkened by the *Föhn* – not only do all these causes interact, they also interact differently according to the inclination and character of the slope, which may be uniform or chaotic, wide open or imprisoned within a gully, or may even consist of a throat at the foot of a continuous or interrupted chimney . . . and so on.

A yard to the right you may be secure, a yard to the left you may sink in or, on the contrary, get no hold at all. The situation often seems baffling, but one of the mountaineer's keenest pleasures is to sense or divine the best way to pick; and this can vary from minute to minute. To some extent the experience is shared by a skier making several runs down the same *piste* in a single day, and encountering different conditions according to the weather, time, sun, wind, temperature and the exposed or sheltered nature of the ground. Higher up it is the same only much more so, because in summer the

sun is hotter and its effects are more violent and because the wind is stronger than on the lower slopes.

In my professional capacity I have climbed Mont Blanc from the Brenva eight times, and conditions were different on every occasion. I have climbed the north face of the Aiguille du Plan six times, two of these ascents being made on successive days; here again, conditions were never the same.

To climb in safety, the mountaineer must keep a careful eye on these continual variations. Even a crampon balling-up because of a sudden change in the snow can cause a slip, a fall and an accident.

Belaying between stances. Make use of rock bollards sticking up out of the ice, after having examined them for strength; put a sufficiently long sling of rope or webbing round them and connect the climbing rope to the sling with a snap-hook. If no bollard is available, put in an ice-screw. Belays of this type are particularly useful when crossing gullies in which falling rocks are a danger, and which must therefore be negotiated quickly.

The leader belayed by the second. The second should first belay himself by pushing his ice-axe in vertically, right up to the head, if the snow is good, that is to say hard and firm; if it is soft he should stamp it down so that when he pushes the ice-axe in it will reach the hard snow beneath.

If the snow is frozen, or if the slope consists of ice, put in an ice-screw.

When crossing a gully it is often feasible to use protruding rocks at the sides of the gully.

Sometimes it is also possible to drive the ice-axe in firmly between the ice and the rock, or to find narrow breaks in the ice into which the ice-axe can be insinuated and wedged; but one must make certain that it is holding well and cannot swivel.

Having belayed himself, the second cuts a step on which he can comfortably stand upright, that is to say well balanced so that he can stand firmly buttressed while supporting himself against the slope. He must be vertically below his self-belaying point.

He then belays the leader exactly as he would on rock, the rope passing round his back or the fold between buttocks and thighs, according to how the leader is climbing. The hand guiding the rope is that nearest the leader.

The stability of the man belaying can be yet further improved by incorporating the ice-axe in such a way as to obtain a three-point basis of support. The rope from the leader passes first round the ice-axe, which has been pushed in as described, then through the directing hand, and from there round the haunches or under the buttocks, and finally to the braking hand. If the leader falls, traction is exerted on a stable structure: namely the climber belaying him, and the ice-axe, on which the belayer can lean with his foot, knee or the hand holding the rope, according to circumstances. Simultaneously, the rope as it runs is gently but effectively braked by the high degree of friction between it and the belayer's clothing.

On very hard snow or on ice, operate as on rock. It is necessary, however, for the second to belay himself to one or several ice-screws.

The stance should not be directly below the leader, nor should the leader climb vertically above it; otherwise, in the event of his slipping or falling, he will come down onto the second.

On the other hand, the stance should be as close as possible to the difficult place (where the leader may be in danger of falling), so that if he does fall he will be stopped as quickly as possible, before he has gathered too much speed.

Finally, as on rock, the Sticht-Salewa brake-plate can be used, provided that two strong belay-points have been secured: an ice-screw for the self-belay, and another for the belay.

The second belayed by the leader. As on rock, there is no impact to be withstood but simply a weight to be held up.

If the snow is good, that is to say if the leader can put his ice-axe in vertically, deeply and firmly, the best method is to belay to the ice-axe, either directly or by way of a sling with a snap-link, through which the climbing rope is passed.

Alternatively, he can face outwards and use a shoulder-belay, after having belayed himself to his ice-axe and cut a comfortable step so as to give himself a firm base; or he can face the slope and belay round his back, putting the rope from the second climber first round the ice-axe, from which it goes to his guiding hand, then round his back, and finally to his controlling hand.

The important thing is that the ice-axe should not come out; to ensure this he can bear on it with his foot, knee or guiding hand.

If the snow is too hard to be penetrated by the shaft of the ice-axe, the leader can drive the blade right in and belay the second to that; but this is makeshift and the security it gives is little more than make-believe.

On very hard snow, and of course on ice, the best method, and even the only reliable one, is to use one or more ice-screws.

Security of the team on the move

On very easy terrain. The rope should always be at stretch, but not absolutely taut. The leader should anticipate any hesitation on the part of the second. The leader (meaning the climber who is highest up) should be the only one to hold coils of rope in his hand; the last coil, as the rope goes down to the second, should end in a turn round the leader's hand, so that if the second man slips, the other coils do not run. If the rope is too long the leader should coil it round his chest and secure it, so as never to have too many coils in his hand.

Some mountaineers put the rope over one shoulder to prevent it from dragging over the snow or rock; a bad habit, because, if the second climber slips, the first is in danger of being thrown off balance and also of being unable to handle the coils.

On easy terrain. The team walks in the ordinary way, with the rope taut and the last loop secured by a turn round the hand; the distance between the climbers should be very short, with the second man following the leader closely when going up, and preceding him by a still shorter distance on the descent. This is precautionary roping. Coming down on snow, on a very steep slope, the leader should make a turn of the rope with a figure-of-eight knot round his ice-axe, which he holds in one hand, and hold the rope in the other, with two loops in reserve.

Moving on a glacier with crevasses. Always go double-roped, the two ropes being of unequal lengths; if one of the climbers falls into a crevasse, this arrangement makes it much simpler to get him out. The procedure is to secure one of the ropes and use it as a fixed rope, while the other is used for belaying; or else both ropes can be used alternately for traction.

The distance between climbers should be fairly long; the leader moves with the rope taut and no loops in reserve; the second has only three or four loops.

The leader can make a knotted loop in the rope, at about arm's length, and hold it in his hand.

1

Belaying to a rock bollard (1).

Shoulder-belay (2).

Leader belaying the second to an ice-piton or ice-screw (3).

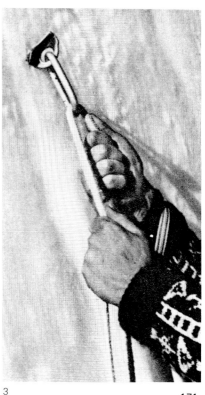

Each climber should have a sling, as long as the distance from his feet to his chest; this sling is put through his harness and the other end is stowed in one of his pockets. It is also a good thing to have one or two ice-screws carried in an easily accessible position.

Moving on an arête with a cornice. Keep well below the possible line of fracture of the cornice. This line is not vertically above the inner, lower border of the cornice; usually, it coincides with the line produced (in the geometrical sense) of the slope which the cornice overhangs.

Moving on a snow arête. If one climber slips and falls down one side of the arête, the best solution for the other climber is to make a glissade down the other side.

How to check a sliding fall. Above all, keep hold of the ice-axe and do not let yourself get suspended on it at arm's length. On the contrary, hold it firmly with both hands round the head and the shaft under one arm, with both arms bent (a very compact, crouching version of the braking position), so that you can use all your weight to anchor the point in the snow.

The feet should be kept (or put) pointing downhill. If the climber is not wearing crampons he can press his toes against the slope for extra braking action. But if wearing crampons, he should not try to use them for braking, as they might check him abruptly, throw him out of position and thus cause the slide to continue; on the contrary, he should raise his feet so that the crampons do not take hold at all, except right at the end, when the slide has almost been brought to a halt.

3

Mountain dangers

Some of the finest mountaineers and some of the best guides, among them Michel Croz, Franz Lochmatter, Emilio Comici, Giusto Gervasutti, Louis Lachenal and Hermann Buhl, have met their deaths in the mountains. Most accidents, however, happen to novices and they occur more often on the way down than on the way up. On rock, accidents are generally individual, while on snow it is more often the whole rope which is involved, the faller dragging the others with him. In mountaineering, unlike most other sports, accidents are often serious. A footballer may slip a cartilage, a skier break a leg; but in mountaineering the slightest mistake may be paid for much more dearly. That is why the rules governing the game must always be kept in mind: sunshine and storm, the dry rock which gives a good hold but also the verglassed rock on which it is so easy to slip, the north wind promising good weather and the west wind presaging storm, the strap that holds and the strap that breaks, the overwhelming heat and, a couple of hours later, the freeze-up at $-5°F$. It is wrong to call the mountains killers: very often it is the climber who, more or less unaware of his error, causes his own death by disregarding the rules or by sheer carelessness. The climber should not be blind to the dangers of the mountains; on the contrary, he should familiarize himself with them and know how to avoid them, or, if he is taken by surprise, to extricate himself safely. To some extent, precautions can now be taken even against lightning (see below).

Dangers are of two kinds: objective, arising from the weather and the mountain itself, and subjective, originating in the climber.

OBJECTIVE DANGERS

Bad rock

The dangers to be guarded against are crumbling rock and falls of stones; often they can be anticipated and avoided.

Crumbling rock. The rock breaks away under the climber's weight or pull. Before it has a chance to do so, test the holds well; do not use brute force; if necessary, distribute the weight of the body over several holds.

Falls of stones. Climbers, frost, thaw, wind or rain may trigger falls of stones in places where the rock is friable; these falls may then sweep down over areas of good rock.

The worst time of day is when the sun is warming up the mountainsides. The stones which were firmly set in the hard snow are no longer held when the snow softens; they slip, fall and sometimes set off other falls. Generally speaking, these falls are canalized in the gullies.

It is therefore important to make an early start and choose the route carefully. Make for ridges rather than gullies.

If a traverse through a danger-zone simply cannot be avoided, one climber starts off while the other, sheltered by a slab or overhang, belays, keeps watch and warns of any impending danger. The climber who is traversing should start by looking to see where the stones are coming from, so as to be able to dodge them.

Not until the last moment should he cover his head with his rucksack or guard it with his arm.

Snow

The commonest dangers are falls into crevasses, and avalanches.

Crevasses and snow bridges. Use the technique already described for moving on snow and ice.

The mountain heights are beautiful, and in the light of the setting sun they appear attractively gentle; here, for example, is Mont Blanc in the colours of the evening. But it must not be forgotten that the mountains hold certain dangers, and the mountaineer must educate himself to know them. One essential is the ability to cope with bad weather, which may strike unexpectedly during a long climb. All these things are part of the rules of the game.

Avalanches

An avalanche is a mass of snow which is set in motion by its own weight and a violent disturbance of its equilibrium. There are two kinds of avalanche: the surface avalanche, in which only the top covering of snow slips, and the ground avalanche, in which the whole mass is carried away.

The formation of avalanches. In summer, there are falls of stones and of ice but relatively few avalanches, because the snow is stabilized. However, an increasing number of climbers are taking to the mountains in spring and even in winter. In addition to an excellent technique this demands a close knowledge of the mountains, because in winter and spring the snow is not stabilized and there is sometimes the danger that an avalanche will occur. The formation of an avalanche depends on the nature of the terrain, the quality of the snow and the temperature.

The nature of the terrain: slippery surfaces. Turf, flattened grass, slabs of shaly rock or smooth rock, under-layers of hard snow or ice, all these are surfaces on which avalanches are likely to occur because the snow does not cling to them.

The contour of the terrain is also important: convex slopes are more dangerous than concave ones which flatten out at the base. Similarly with the incline: any slope of under 15 degrees is safe, provided it is not dominated by steeper slopes. Snow slabs are dangerous above 15 degrees; fresh snows (powdery and wet) are dangerous from 25 degrees; compressed powder snows, and spring snows, are safe up to 30 degrees; hard snows are safe on all inclines.

The nature of the snow. Instability increases with the thickness of the covering, but also according to the quality of the snow. Fresh snows (powdery, wet and moist) and snows which do not adhere (powder snow on ice, moist snow on a wet base) are the most unstable.

The temperature. When the temperature rises the snow humidifies and becomes heavy, and therefore unstable. Cold, on the other hand, stabilizes it by causing the crystals to interlock. In summer, after a fall of fresh snow, one should wait two or three days before setting out on a climb, to give the snow time to become stabilized. During these three days the danger increases if the snow softens again (because of rain or the *Föhn*).

How avalanches are triggered off

Avalanches often fall at regular times, but they sometimes start unexpectedly, becoming detached by a sudden disturbance of their mechanical or thermal equilibrium.

Failure of mechanical equilibrium. This may be caused by the passage of a climber or skier, particularly if he is traversing the slope; the overloading of a slope by several climbers or skiers; the fall of a cornice, or falling séracs or stones; or vibrations of the atmosphere, caused by wind, loud noise or the blast of other avalanches. These indications are particularly true of powdery snows.

Failure of thermal equilibrium. This comes with thawing, through loss of cohesion between crystals; or when the snow freezes again, making the mass contract and crack, a process which often begins promptly at sunset.

Principal types of avalanche

Avalanche of powdery snow. This is especially a winter avalanche, occurring on steep slopes after a fresh fall of snow. There has to be

Snow-bridges are particularly frail in autumn, when the snow-covering is still fairly thin and has not had time to become stabilized. Below: the crevasse into which Louis Lachenal fell, in the Vallée Blanche.

Right: the great avalanche which nearly carried away Camp 2, on Annapurna.

some sort of violent shock for it to become detached, such as a very strong wind, the blast of another avalanche or the fall of a cornice or of a climber.

It flies along in eddying clouds and is extremely fast. It is preceded by a violent gust of wind and makes a deafening noise. An avalanche of powder snow is capable of flattening quite a large tract of woodland and, because of its blast, may even cause destruction on the opposite slope. It can kill a mountaineer by suffocation, because the snow enters the bronchial tubes. If caught in this way, the climber should turn his back to the oncoming avalanche and protect his nose and mouth.

Avalanche of fresh wet snow. This is often a surface avalanche, but its weight may make it a ground avalanche. It is very much affected by thermal conditions and is the type of avalanche which falls during warm periods when the snow softens. It moves a little slower than the avalanche of powder snow.

It rolls, but makes a powerful blast none the less; its consequences are the same as those of the powder-snow variety, but it has in addition a crushing effect because of its weight. On coming to a halt it hardens immediately, like plaster.

A climber caught in an avalanche of this type should try to stay on the surface by making swimming movements, and should strive to disengage himself before the snow solidifies.

Avalanche of wet snow. This is predominantly a springtime avalanche and nearly always a ground avalanche. It may also fall in winter when there is rain. The sun, the *Föhn*, the rain or contraction at the time of refreezing–any of these may be the cause of its breaking away. It is fairly predictable, usually happening in the same places each year.

It flows slowly but its force is considerable: it flattens and destroys everything. The climber should avoid the gullies down which it habitually descends. One cubic metre of powder snow weighs about two pounds; the same volume of wet snow weighs nearly a ton.

Snow-slab avalanche. This is a very dangerous avalanche because it is often unforeseeable. A snow-slab is made of snow which is superficially compressed but has not adhered to the underlying layer, from which it remains separated by a layer of air. It is usually found on one side of a ridge, often when the latter is surmounted by a cornice. Snow-slabs are particularly to be feared after a fall of fresh snow, for then they are no longer visible. They are in any case difficult to recognize: of a dull, yellowish white colour and a dense consistency.

They are noisy; they make a hollow sound because they form a sort of vault over the under-layer and the air-gap between. They are especially dangerous in winter. In spring, they become gradually compressed and finally stick to the under-layer. What sets them in motion is a breakdown of mechanical equilibrium.

They slide. The climber should be very careful in places where they might occur, particularly after a fresh fall of snow.

Cornice avalanche. It is largely in winter and spring that cornices constitute a danger; in summer they are more stabilized, though always somewhat precarious.

Sérac avalanches. These are caused by the movement of the glacier and may occur at any time. The climber should move very quickly when crossing an exposed area.

Snow-slab avalanche on the Weissfluh.

Rules to observe in avalanche zones. Move on the ridges rather than in the coombs; go above snow-slabs, not below them; use the edges and not the bed of gullies; keep wide intervals, and mount slopes directly rather than in traverse.

Before crossing an avalanche zone, make sure you know what to do should you become involved: do not let go of your ice-axe; try to get to the edge, making swimming movements to help you to keep on the surface; if you find yourself being rolled along in the avalanche, do not lose your awareness of which way up you are and, before the avalanche stops, strive to keep your head (or failing this, an arm) up in the air, especially if you are covered by the snow. Never passively surrender; keep fighting all the time.

Bad weather

This may take various forms.

Storm. This is the combined action of wind, cold, rain, mist, snow and sometimes thunder and lightning. All footprints are obliterated, the snow penetrates everywhere and the mountaineer feels utterly lost. In these circumstances he should think clearly, calmly and very quickly, in order to make a wise decision which will take into account the terrain, the time of day, the changes occurring on the mountain and the physical and mental state of the party. Whatever happens, he must not stop and sleep.

Mist. This may come up even in fine weather. It is more dangerous on a glacier than on rock because of the absence of landmarks.

Warm wind (Föhn). This softens the snow and may therefore start avalanches and weaken snow-bridges over crevasses.

Thunderstorms and lightning. There is a great deal still to be discovered about these electrical phenomena. However, Alvin E. Peterson, an electrical engineer who works for the United States Bureau of Standards, has published in the *American Alpine Journal* a substantial and extremely useful study which is capable of saving the lives of many climbers in dangerous circumstances. Mr H. Adams Caster, editorial director of the *A.A.J.*, and Mr Peterson himself, have very kindly allowed me to reproduce extracts from this study; I wish to thank both them and Pierre Henry and Jacques Tessier du Cros, who made the French translation which appeared in *La Montagne*, the journal of the French Alpine Club.

Protective measures against lightning:

1. The best way to avoid being struck by lightning in the mountains is not to stay on exposed summits or arêtes, or a flat open place, during an electric storm. Whenever a thunderstorm is clearly imminent, it is only common sense not to go climbing.

2. If you find yourself in an exposed place, with time to spare before the storm reaches you, come down as fast as you can and do your best to keep away from exposed ridges. In particular, keep away from any spur or other protruding feature. The middle of an arête is preferable to its tip. A rubble-strewn slope lower down, with a small block to sit on, is a good refuge, provided it does not constitute an eminence rising above a smooth site surrounding it. Tall or isolated trees are also to be avoided.

3. If lightning appears to be imminent or is already striking nearby, lose no time but find a place protected both from direct strikes and from ground currents. A ledge, a slope or even a slight eminence, if dominated by a high point in its proximity, is more or less proof against a direct strike. The place where you crouch for shelter should be at least a yard, preferably more, away from any vertical rock; the height of the latter should be at least from

Fall of séracs, producing an avalanche of ice-dust and snow, on the Trugberg, in the Bernese Oberland.

Paths of powerful ground currents caused by a lightning-strike higher up.

Do not linger under an overhang or at the foot of a vertical crack.

Possible point of strike

A boulder-strewn slope is comparatively safe

Keep away from large isolated blocks

Crack down which water can flow

Belay at right-angles to ground current

No !

five to ten times greater than that of yourself in the crouching position, and the distance between yourself and the foot of the vertical feature should be no greater than the latter's height.

In the vicinity of a sharp point of rock, the minimum safety distance is 15 yards downhill, preferably further. If possible, choose a dry spot, without lichen, or a slope strewn with rock-rubble. Avoid the proximity of rising cracks containing earth or moisture, likewise anfractuosities and caves, unless they are roomy enough to let you sit more than a yard away from the walls with the roof 10 feet above your head. A cave may well be the terminus of a crack coming from above and conducting water; this is a major source of danger. Another place to avoid is the mouth of a hollow in the rock; closing a gap of this kind is risky. In a thunderstorm, the sense of safety given by an overhang or small cave is deceptive. Also to be avoided is sitting in a hole or depression the edges of which are less than a yard or a yard and a half apart; the discharge is quite capable of leaping the gap and passing through the body.

4. A crouching position, or a sitting position with knees raised and feet together, seems best; the smaller the distances between the points at which contact is made with the ground, the greater the safety. Any position should be carefully avoided in which the head or torso is between the points of contact; in particular, do not touch the rock wall with hand, shoulder or head.

5. You are recommended to insulate yourself from the rock or earth by means of any insulating material you happen to have with you. A coil of nylon rope is excellent if it is dry, and good even if it is wet. A porter's wooden carrying frame can also be used, a pair of boots or shoes with crêpe soles (without nails), a rubberized cape, a folded sleeping bag or outer garment, a rucksack or a folded woollen shirt. Dry objects are always better than wet ones, and if it is raining it is a good thing to keep both your skin and your clothes dry by wearing a cape.

The metal frame of a rucksack, laid flat on the ground, can be used provided you can sit on it without overlapping it, because ground currents will be conducted by it rather than by your body. A flat rock just wide enough to accommodate you, including your feet, also makes a good seat, provided it is separate from the surrounding earth or rock formation or is situated on a slope of boulders or scree.

6. A climber caught in a storm on an escarpment, and in danger of falling if he loses consciousness or is attacked by cramp, should belay himself. A nylon safety rope is better than one of hemp or cotton. The point of attachment should be close, so as to reduce the potential gradient along the rope; and there should be a little slack, to increase insulation. It is preferable to rope round the ankles rather than the waist, and in any case not under the armpits.

7. On open ground, as already advised, seek the protected zone away from any protuberant feature; failing this, sit down and huddle yourself as small as you can.

8. When a storm is imminent, the benefits of roping-down are speculative; they belong to the realm of probability calculus rather than ordinary foresight. Roping-down may be the quickest means of getting out of a danger-zone. The risk is minimal if the rope is made of nylon and is dry, and provided the climber comes down with his feet together and does not make contact with the rock with anything but his feet.But a discharge could make him let go.

9. The author disagrees utterly with the common belief that climbers should get rid of their ice-axes, pitons and other metallic

objects when a discharge appears to be imminent. Their presence adds little or nothing to the electrical danger, and later, on wet, slippery going, one might regret being without them. Metal does not in itself 'attract electricity'; the climber's body, being higher and having less electrical resistance, is more likely to act as a lightning-conductor than is an ice-axe. Observations made with two ordinary ice-axes, with wooden shafts, showed a resistance of at least 500,000 ohms between head and point when wet, and 1,000 times more than this when dry; thus the shaft of an ice-axe has a resistance between 100 and 5,000 times greater than that of a climber's body. Moreover, its resistance when wet is increased by a coat of wax or linseed oil.

The ice-axe should not be waved over the head. If carried normally, it adds nothing to the danger. The best thing is to lay it down flat, and to put your pitons into your rucksack or lay them on the ground a short distance away from you.

10. Nothing has been said about the composition of the terrain and its possible effects; the author's view is that it has no influence, except perhaps to a very minor degree. For example, variations in the resistance of the surface of the ground or rock are unimportant compared with the magnitude of the discharge and the proximity of its point of impact.

In conclusion, the danger from lightning in the mountains varies according to circumstance.

If caught in a storm, react promptly: do your best to avoid a direct strike and its effects, insulate yourself from the ground, and position yourself in such a way as not to offer a favourable path to the currents running momentarily in the surface of the rocks and along cracks; belay yourself if a shock could cause you to fall – and don't lose your ice-axe! Merely sitting on a coil of rope, a yard away from a rockface instead of leaning against it, may be enough to keep you out of the statistics of deaths by lightning.

Rain. This makes rock and ice very slippery.

Darkness. This is not really a danger, but because of factors like cold, situation and the climber's state of fatigue it can be a cause of accidents. Try to organize the best possible bivouac before darkness becomes complete.

Sun. This can burn the skin and eyes and may also affect the climber's general condition (by causing weakness and lassitude).

SUBJECTIVE DANGERS

These have their origin in the mountaineer himself. Many factors may be involved: lack of training, causing nervous and muscular fatigue (particularly on the way down); lack of knowledge of snow and rock, errors in route-finding, delays, faulty estimation of conditions or of the difficulty of a certain pitch or route, technical and physical incapacity – which results in making an over-ambitious plan and not giving it up soon enough; the momentary loss of concentration which throws a climber off balance; the slip or stumble, the snow which balls up on the feet, the foot badly placed in a step, a sudden movement, perhaps to retrieve a slipping piton; equipment which is defective, or inadequate for the project in hand.

To combat subjective dangers, which in fact means combating oneself, there is only one answer: one must have good muscles, but it matters even more to have a good head. Mountaineering calls for considerable physical powers – strength, skill, stamina – but these will be worth nothing if they are not used intelligently.

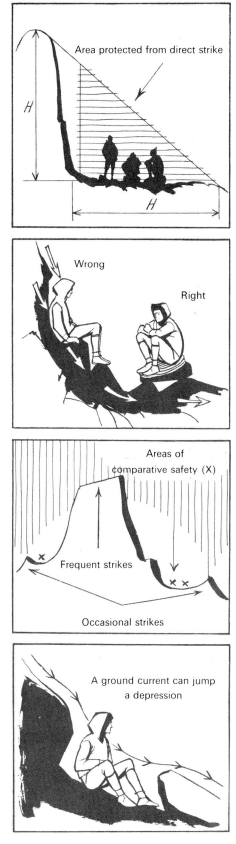

The project

During winter and spring, mountaineering projects mature in the mind of the climber rather like fruits on a tree. A project is not only a succession of cracks, slabs and chimneys, it is first and foremost a voice which summons, the name of a peak which resounds in the heart; it then becomes an enterprise which involves the climber's whole being.

During my early years of mountaineering I did not have the good fortune to live in Chamonix. The enchanted world of the high peaks was not constantly before my eyes; so every day I looked through mountaineering books and journals, ranging from accounts of expeditions, which thrilled me, to the dry, technical sections which were hard reading. The photographs interested me even more than the text. I studied them at length, training myself to recognize the peaks they depicted. I did not read the captions till afterwards and was always happy if I had recognized the summit of the Aiguille Verte or the sheer drop of the Grépon, and disappointed if I had guessed wrong. Some of the photographers in town specialized in mountain pictures, and I used to pass back and forth in front of the window displays, gazing. Now that I live in Chamonix I can see the whole range from my chalet, but familiarity has rubbed none of the bloom off it. Before thinking of actually climbing I abandon myself to contemplation, and while, under the influence of the weather, time of day and light, the mountains are revealing facets hitherto unknown to me, details hitherto unperceived, reactions hitherto unsuspected, I muse and dream; the high places know so well how to keep their mysteries intact! I have climbed nearly every peak in the massif, yet I have often found that any of them can still provide a new experience – even a trifling difference may effect the transformation. They are not dead or inanimate, they are always playing with wind and snow, sunshine and darkness. They sparkle with light or crackle with cold; an intense but secret life exists up there, and I take part in it with the whole of my being.

A climb taking shape. First, you simply want to make a certain climb; then you start translating desire into preparation. The projected ascent *must* be within the climber's abilities; this is categorical. He must not set himself too hard a climb – he would only struggle in vain and might quickly get put off from what is in fact a marvellous sport. At best, he will find it only relatively satisfying and will at the same time be risking an accident.

An expedition begins long before you actually start out. Preparing for a climb is always fun. First there is the training – climbing, walking and perhaps physical exercises and, at the same time, the study of the project in view. The mountaineer should be, as far as possible, familiar with every expedition before he undertakes it: he must know the exact position of the summit, the route he hopes to take and the alternative routes; he must evaluate the conditions and inform himself of the difficulties, including any danger-sources (falls of stones at a given time of day in a particular place, and the influence of orientation on the rock, which may be warm, cold or ice-covered). An accumulation of small items of information is sometimes the key to success where a big climb is concerned. Preparation takes various forms: studying the map; reading guide-books, works on mountaineering, accounts of climbs and technical notes; looking at photographs; consulting friends who have already made the projected ascents.

I remember that before I knew much about the mountains I used

Conditions on snow and ice are much more changeable than on rock. Here, the snow has been carved by the wind. On crust strong enough to take the climber's weight, progress is easy; on breakable crust, difficult. And the climber must be on his guard against snow-slabs formed by the wind; they are sometimes highly dangerous.

On the terrace of the Couvercle hut; from left to right: Georges Tairraz, Gaston Rébuffat, René Claret-Tournier (who has climbed Mont Blanc more than 300 times), Anderl Heckmair (first ascent of the north face of the Eiger) and Hermann Buhl (first ascent of Nanga Parbat).

to spend whole days studying a massif and preparing for a season's climbing. There is something wonderful about reading a map; what dreams and plans it conjures up!

Also think about who is to go with you. To me, this is as important as the climb itself.

The beginner's introduction to the mountains will be effected through a guide, or a friend acting in that capacity. He will make ascents, but if he wants to become a real mountaineer, he must not make reaching the summit his whole aim; he must use his eyes and mind, deliberately learn through curiosity and experience. He may have engaged a professional, but that is no reason for ignoring the practical problems of the ascent; on the contrary, he can and should ask the guide sometimes to let him move up and become No. 1 on the rope. One rarely or never sees a client going in front of his guide; people have fixed ideas about guides, regarding them as professionals who, for a certain sum, lead or escort their clients to a summit. But a guide is more than that; he is a friend with the ability to inspire confidence and interest, enabling others to share the beauties of his own domain. The guide is happy when the climber he takes with him is happy.

The mountain hut. Try to get there early enough to rest and get the most out of a pleasant evening. If visiting the area for the first time, study the map and get your bearings. Sometimes you will need to go out and reconnoitre by daylight the ground you will be covering in darkness when you set off in the small hours of the following morning. Have a good supper, prepare the equipment required for the climb, leave the rest of your things tidy and go quietly to bed.

The ascent. Get up early. Fix a timetable and try to stick to it. One seldom regrets an early start but one always regrets having started too late; primarily for reasons of safety ('it is later than you think' is nowhere so true as on a mountain), but also because of the strange beauty of the moment: daylight is preparing to supplant darkness – soon the peaks will be lit up, there is hope as well as mystery in the air. Setting out with a lamp strapped to your forehead may seem hard, but it is wonderful too. Then comes dawn, the birth of a new day, and in making your way up your mountain you climb to meet the sun.

If you are making a snow climb, starting on a very cold night followed by a very cold morning, and if you are wearing crampons, do not forget to wriggle your toes from time to time to make sure they have not gone numb.

During the climb there will be no question of hurrying; equally, though, you must not waste time; once on the summit you will want time to look about you at leisure. What unnecessarily prolongs a climb, making it tedious and in some cases dangerous, is dawdling and making frequent halts without good reason. If rucksacks and ropes are handled competently, and belays are effected with correct technique, every manoeuvre will flow smoothly and automatically, avoiding delay and, most important of all, maintaining that regular rhythm which minimizes fatigue and is in itself a considerable pleasure. Nevertheless, climbers should also be capable of moving fast, even very fast, for example when crossing a gully where avalanches are frequent, or when a storm is imminent. Weather and other conditions change so quickly at high altitudes that there are times when safety increases in direct proportion to speed.

It is important to ration one's energies and to know just when and where in the course of the climb the difficult pitches will be encountered, so as to attack them in good form. Thanks to the classification of difficulties into six grades, the climber can avail himself of accurate information, relating to dry rock, concerning the difficulty of the various pitches. The purpose of this classification is limited: it is

The Aiguilles de Chamonix.

meant to improve the standard of technical notes and of guidebooks. Whereas pitches used to be described as severe, rather severe, very severe, dangerous, exposed, or difficult, indications are now more succinct: a pitch will be described, for example, as Grade IV. (The Alpine Grades of difficulty are I, II, III, IV, V and VI for Free Climbing and A1, A2 and A3 for Artificial Climbing; some Alpine climbs have a combination of Free and Artificial pitches and these are double-graded, e.g. IV A1.) The climber thus has an indication which, though not perfect, is more exact than the old one and enables him to draw comparisons with pitches he has already climbed. To render such comparisons valid, all classifications refer exclusively to dry rock.

Throughout the expedition the climber must interpret the mountain: plot his course according to the terrain; put on crampons or take them off, not because somebody's technical treatise tells him to but because the state of the snow or ice demands it. He must note the various conditions: *névé* snow hardened by the frost, then softened by the sun to varying degrees determined by orientation; ice on steep places; *soufflée* snow in cols swept by the wind, and so on. The climber is a composer: with each length of rope he is, as it were, building his mountain.

It pays to imagine what the projected climb would be like in the event of bad weather, with clouds obscuring the west, filling the valley and gradually rising to envelop the rope of climbers, isolating them in the mist and cold.

It is dangerous for a novice to go to the limit of his capacity; the stage for this will not be reached until he has had several seasons of climbing and has acquired plenty of experience. With that stage as his goal, he might consider every climb as an examination, though of course without letting this interfere with his emotional and aesthetic enjoyment. I would suggest a log-book in which the climber records: date of the ascent; summit climbed; route followed; conditions; difficulties encountered; time-table; members of the team.

In addition, he can try marking himself on: confidence, decision, coolness; ability in route-finding; belaying, and handling the rope; physical capacity; ability on rock; ability on ice.

The marks are bound to be arbitrary, but one must try to award them fairly. I doubt if the marking on handling the rope (didn't it drag along on the snow sometimes?) will always be 20 out of 20. And did the council of war always take the best decisions, and adopt the best route?

The novice should make his way up from each standard of climbing ability to the next. If I advise him to mark himself, as we do in the guides' courses, it is so that he may regard each expedition not only as an examination but also as a grading of his progress. An ascent which has been successfully made as second behind a guide may be repeated the following year as first on a second rope following a team with a guide, and as leader two or three years later. It is satisfying to make ascents of increasing difficulty for one's own pleasure, but it should be remembered that to initiate others is also one of the greatest joys that mountaineering can afford.

Choosing climbs, and advancing from the easier ones to the harder, is a matter for the conscience of the individual climber. Some ascents are difficult but popular; others are easier but little-known, forcing one to find one's own way and helping to transform the climber into a mountaineer. The characteristic feature of the granite massifs is their geometric structure; the detailed route, which is fairly easy to find, is determined by the systems of major fractures. In other massifs the climber will have to be continually searching, trying out holds which are frequently more numerous than in granite but often hidden, irregular, distorted, inverted. Such holds have to be used in the right direction: a doubtful hold, which would, as it were, come out like a drawer if gripped in the wrong direction, will prove serviceable if gripped at right-angles to its axis. On limestone, in particular, pitches can rarely be tackled directly; you have to use your wits, be inquisitive, go to the right, come back again, try to the left, traverse.

Halfway through a climb it is good to halt for a while, perhaps for lunch, then on and up to the summit for a well-earned rest.

The descent should not begin too late, especially if the route includes a good deal of snow; there must always be a safety margin. A typical case is the Whymper couloir on the Aiguille Verte: as soon as the sun has come round to it and warmed it up it becomes tricky and sometimes dangerous to cross; the softened snow is insecure and is liable to avalanche.

If one has climbed a summit by a difficult route, it is wise to be sure of the descent route in advance and not to relax one's vigilance until safely back in the hut. If roping down is involved, do not tense yourself on the ropes; the abseil should always be a pleasure as well as a fast, safe method of descent.

As the approach march from the valley to the hut is usually the least interesting part of the expedition, it is a good idea, if you have the energy, to make several ascents from the same hut.

If the weather is dubious, I would urge the climber not to hang about doing nothing but to undertake some simple climb which is devoid of objective dangers. In this book I have frequently under-lined the most important factor in our sport: safety. If I now suggest that the mountaineer set out in uncertain weather it is not from any desire to see him wantonly expose himself to the elements; far from it. It is simply that bad weather is something with which he ought to familiarize himself before it becomes a danger.

He should therefore train himself to assess changes in the weather and see that he knows what to do before and during a thunderstorm. Then, in due course, he will be able to set out for longer, harder climbs with the vital sense of confidence that he can come through them safely, even in bad weather.

Doubtful weather can also be used for ice-training. Whereas a good deal of rock-training can be done near a town, opportunities for training in step-cutting and the use of crampons are rare. Here is a suggested programme:

1. Crampon practice, climbing, descending, traversing, both individually and on the rope, choosing steeper and steeper slopes.

2. Step-cutting practice, either stopping to cut each step or cutting them on the move, holding the ice-axe with the right hand, the left hand or both.

3. Negotiating bergschrunds, both climbing up and jumping down; practice in glissading with the ice-axe on steep slopes, and without it on gentle ones; and finally, on a slope with a flat place at the bottom, learn to fall, gain control and come to a stop; and practise running belays.

If visibility is poor, it will be profitable to take map and compass, work out your direction and 'navigate' in the mist. Do not wait to be nonplussed at 13,000 feet before learning how to find your way by compass.

And if the weather is too bad for anything else you can always clean out the hut—this, too, is part of the mountaineer's job!

The time spent at a hut is one of the pleasantest things about a climb. Above, left: the old Couvercle hut; below, left: the Nissen-type hut on the Col de Jorasses; right: the Solvay hut, on the Hornli arête of the Matterhorn.

The kingdom of light and silence

The mountains come to life because men love them, as at least one beginner has guessed; and their many beauties are intensified by a young climber's fervour. Technique must be the servant of enthusiasm, otherwise it reduces the world of the heights to the proportion of a gymnasium. It is a long road that leads to the peaks. Up there, where human habitation and then the trees and finally even the grass disappear, the barren kingdom begins – inanimate, wild, savage and yet, in its extreme poverty and utter nakedness, able to bestow a wealth beyond price: the happiness in the eyes of those who frequent it.

The mountaineer must have strong muscles, fingers of steel and a perfect technique; but all these are only tools. Above all he loves life; and at 13,000 feet the air has a special savour. But this savour has to be earned. Though people nowadays are becoming daily more content with easy satisfactions, man should remain demanding – he should ask much of himself, for he cannot love the kind of peace which is merely the absence of life and vitality. 'Where there's a will there's a way.' It is not enough for man to exist, he must live. Not live dangerously, however; that is easy and, in a sense, corrupt. He is both body and soul, and the high peaks invite him to action and contemplation, enabling him to revive the fires of forgotten dreams.

But the beauty of the mountain-tops, the freedom of enormous spaces, the hard and simple joys of climbing, the rediscovery of nature and of our kinship with it, would be unsatisfying and would sometimes leave a bitter taste in the mouth were it not for the comradeship of the rope – a brotherly affection born of considerateness, dedication and the sharing of both struggle and joy.

I often think of Moulin and how he initiated me. I have now made slightly over a thousand ascents, at all seasons, and sometimes I have the feeling that the mountains are my kingdom. And yet every time I penetrate the barriers surrounding them, barriers which the eye cannot see but which I nevertheless sense very clearly, I am aware of a slight tremor within myself.

Moulin, years ago, was the one who 'knew'; and now, like him, I 'know'. But even if I had climbed all the summits in the world, by every possible route, I would still not know everything about this world that I love. I shall always be on my way for there will always be something new.

187

The Campanile di Val Montanaia.

PHOTOGRAPHIC CREDITS

Most of the illustrations in this book are by Gabriel Ollive. The others are by Maurice Baquet, Pierre Bonnant, René Caloz, Edouard Frendo, Ghedina, Jean Guillemin, Maurice Jarnoux, Jean-Jacques Languepin, René Mallieux, Janine Niepce, Pierre Périchon, Bernard Pierre, Gaston Rébuffat, André Roch, Georges and Pierre Tairraz.

The photos on pp. 42, 46, 48 and 50 are by René Bonnardel.